Riders

of the

Pony Express

RALPH MOODY

Illustrated by Robert Riger

maps by Leonard Derwinski

University of Nebraska Press
Lincoln and London

First Nebraska paperback printing: 2004

Library of Congress Cataloging-in-Publication Data
Moody, Ralph, 1898–
Riders of the Pony express / Ralph Moody; illustrated by Robert
Riger; maps by Leonard Derwinski.—1st Nebraska paperback.
p.   cm.
Originally published: Boston: Houghton Mifflin, 1958.
ISBN 0-8032-8305-9 (pbk.: alk. paper)—ISBN 0-8032-3249-7
(hardcover: alk. paper)
1. Pony express.   2. Express service—United States.
I. Riger, Bob.   II. Title.
HE6375.P65M66   2004
383'.143'0973—dc22
2004004978

This Bison Books edition follows the original in beginning chapter
1 on arabic page 13; the text remains unaltered.

CONTENTS

Riders

of the

Pony Express

1

WHEN GOLD was discovered at Sutter's mill the
news had barely stirred a ripple in San Francisco,
but April 3, 1860, was a day of wild excitement,
joy, and celebration. A shouting crowd jammed
Montgomery Street from gutter to gutter. Frightened horses bolted away, upsetting carriages and
unseating riders.

The people of San Francisco had reason to
celebrate. Their fastest means of communication
with the East had been letters carried by stage-
coach on the Butterfield Overland Mail route,
and the trip took nearly a month. Now a rider,
mounted on a swift horse, was ready to race
away on the 1966-mile run to St. Joseph, Missouri,

with the first Pony Express mail. If, as promised, the run could be made in ten days, Californians would for the first time be in close touch with news of the nation and their friends and relatives in the East. But the Pony Express had been established for a far greater reason than to furnish the Californians this convenience.

The embers of civil war were smoldering, and slaveholding states were threatening to secede from the Union. Although California had been admitted to the Union as a free state, its loyalty was very doubtful. Many of its citizens and government officials were from the South and were determined to swing the Golden State to the Confederacy. There was a great possibility of their success. Less than 500 miles separated California from the slaveholding state of Texas, but nearly 2000 miles of wilderness and high mountains cut it off from the closest free state to the east. In addition, the Butterfield Overland Mail route lay entirely through the South, where Union communications to California could be cut at any time.

The President and supporters of the Union

were deeply worried. In case of war, the loss of California with its fabulous wealth might be a staggering blow to the Union cause. If the state were to be saved, a faster and safer means of communication with loyal California Unionists must be established immediately.

One of America's greatest strengths is her ability to produce men capable of meeting every national emergency. The man who rose to meet this one was William Russell. He was the senior partner of Russell, Majors & Waddell, overland freighters between St. Joseph, Missouri, and Salt Lake City, Utah. He believed that by a central route light riders on relays of fast horses could carry the mail between St. Joseph and San Francisco in ten days. From St. Joseph it could be speeded east by the newly built railroad.

At first everyone laughed at Mr. Russell's idea. Mountain men argued that the Rockies and Sierra Nevadas could never be successfully crossed in winter. Plainsmen argued that the Sioux and Paiute Indians would kill any lone rider trying to cross their homelands.

Mr. Russell still remained firm in his belief.

He knew the western country thoroughly, and he knew the type of lightweight, hard-riding young horsemen it was producing. He was sure that 80 of the best among them, with 400 fast horses, could overcome every obstacle with speed, courage, and determination.

To do the job, 80 well-supplied relay stations would have to be built along the most direct route — across the prairies and up the Platte and Sweetwater Rivers to South Pass, through rugged Utah, around Great Salt Lake, across the Nevada deserts and over the high Sierra Nevada Mountains of California. To guard the stations from Indian attack, and to provide food and shelter for riders and horses, 200 keepers and stablemen would be needed.

Mr. Russell knew the cost would be tremendous, but he offered to furnish the United States Government semiweekly, ten-day Pony Express mail service between St. Joseph and San Francisco for $500 a round trip.

When in January, 1860, Mr. Russell made his offer, the Senate was sharply divided between pro-slavery and anti-slavery forces. Southern senators were determined that Northern communications with California should not be improved. They were successful in blocking passage of a bill to pay for the carrying of Pony Express mail.

When the Senate refused to pay for their services, Mr. Russell and his partners decided that they had an obligation to their country, and would discharge it regardless of cost to themselves. They immediately set to work, making careful plans for speeding and safeguarding the Pony Mail. They believed that both depended on the swiftness and endurance of relay ponies, since a single rider could not fight off Indian attacks and would have to escape them by running away. For this reason, a pony's load must be no more than 165 pounds. Only riders weighing 120 pounds or less would be hired, equipment must weigh no more than 25 pounds, and each rider's mail load would be limited to 20 pounds.

To reduce weight, protect the mail, and speed up relays, Mr. Russell had special Pony Express saddles and *mochilas* made. The saddle was only a light wooden frame, with horn, cantle, stirrups, and bellyband. The *mochila* (pronounced "mo-chee'-la"), or mantle, was an easily removable leather cover that fitted over the saddle, with openings to let the horn and cantle stick through. At each corner of the *mochila* there was a cantina, or pouch, for carrying mail. These were fitted with locks, and the keys would be kept only at Salt Lake City, San Francisco, and St. Joseph.

Each *mochila* would be carried the full length of the line, being moved from pony to pony as relays were made. Since the rider would be sitting on it, it could not be lost or stolen while he was mounted. If he were to be thrown or killed during his run, the *mochila* would remain on the saddle and, no doubt, be carried on to the next relay station by the riderless pony.

Mr. Russell knew every foot of the 1966-mile Pony Express trail, and divided it carefully into

relays for the ponies and routes for the riders. Where the going would not be too hard for a pony, relay stations were spaced 25 to 30 miles apart. Where the country was rugged they were spaced nearer together. Each rider was given from three to five relays in his route. At both ends he would have a "home station" where he would live between runs.

Every trip made with the Pony Express mail would be a race against time. In addition, Mr. Russell made them races between the California and Mormon riders west of the Rockies and the prairie riders on the eastern side. Keen rivalry already existed, and he took full advantage of it in setting schedules and buying horses, doing his best to make the race an even one.

For the rugged mountains and deserts west of the Rockies, he had tough mustangs bought, and set the schedule at 165 miles a day. For the prairie riders he had many fast race horses purchased, and set the schedule at 220 miles a day. The prairie boys must ride considerably faster than the Westerners, but they would be following the Oregon Trail most of the way, and would have no high mountains to cross. Of course, there could be no finish line, for the race would start at both ends of the route. But whichever team was first to reach Bear River, on the Utah-Wyoming boundary, would be the winner.

With their plans made, the partners wasted no time. They announced that Pony Express mail service would start from both San Francisco and St. Joseph at five o'clock on the afternoon of April 3. Then they sent the best men in their employ out to build relay stations, purchase hay and grain, buy the finest horses that could be secured at any price — and to find young men who were worthy of carrying their country's mail.

The West was full of rough, daring, and reckless gunmen who were afraid of nothing and could be hired for $30 a month. Russell, Majors & Waddell would have none of them. They would pay their Pony Express riders $100 to $150 a month, but no man would be entrusted to carry the mail until he had signed this pledge:

I do hereby swear, before the Great and Living God, that during my engagement, and while I am an employe of Russell, Majors & Waddell, I will, under no circumstances, use profane language; that I will drink no intoxicating liquors; that I will not quarrel or fight with any other employe of the firm, and that in every respect I will conduct myself honestly, be faithful to my duties, and so direct all my acts as to win the confidence of my employers. So help me God.

As each rider was hired, he was given a light-weight rifle, a Colt revolver, a bright red flannel shirt, blue trousers, a horn, and a Bible. Each man was assigned to the part of the long trail that he knew best, and was given a few simple instructions.

In spite of weather, lack of rest, or personal danger to himself, the mail must go through. Whenever a *mochila* was brought in, he must immediately carry it over his route at the fastest speed his mounts could endure. Two minutes would be allowed for changing ponies at relay stops. To carry mail on schedule was his duty; to carry it safely was his trust. Whenever possible, he must avoid Indian fights, depending on his pony's speed to make an escape. The uniform might be worn or not, as the rider chose. If he wished, he might carry an extra revolver instead of a rifle.

Although the task seemed impossible, everything was in readiness by the afternoon of April 3. Twilight was just falling in San Francisco when the Pony Express agent locked the first St. Joseph mail into the cantinas. As the crowd whistled and shrieked, Jim Randall tossed the *mochila* over his saddle, swung aboard, and raced away on a beautiful Palomino pony.

Actually, Jim and the Palomino were no more than showpieces. Their run would be only to the wharf, where they would go aboard the steamer *Antelope* and ride quietly up the river to Sacramento. From there, the actual race was scheduled to start at midnight, and rough, tough Sam Hamilton would be the first real Pony Rider eastward.

Johnny Frey, the First Rider

2

IN 1860, St. Joseph was a sprawling frontier town on the muddy banks of the Missouri River, and its send-off of the first Pony Express rider was even wilder than San Francisco's.

A late train — and a few nearby saloons — helped the celebration along. By five o'clock on April 3, a big crowd of frontiersmen had gathered in front of the Pony Express office, but the mail train from the East was more than two hours late. The crowd was thirsty, and Jeff Thompson, the colorful and popular Mayor, was full of oratory. With so long a wait, the frontiersmen quenched their thirst often, and with each drink their cheers grew louder.

The Mayor would not be outdone. As the noise of the crowd increased, he raised his voice to a bull-like bellow. After introducing Mr. Russell and his business partner, Mr. Majors, he talked on and on, until the train came in, and he ended in a burst of flowery phrases and waving arms.

"The mail must go through," he shouted. "Hurled by flesh and blood across two thousand miles of desolate space . . . neither storms, fatigue, darkness, mountains or Indians, burning sand or snow must stop the precious bags. The mail must go!"

The mail did go, but less than half of the crowd knew who carried it. Just as the mail train pulled in, Bill Richardson, a hostler at the livery stable, rode up on the bay mare that was to make the first Pony Express run. By this time it was growing dark, torches had been lighted, and the crowd was in a wild uproar. A newspaper reporter, anxious to be first out with the news, rushed back to his office and wrote the thrilling story of Bill's grand take-off, but it was a young man named Johnny Frey who carried the first Pony Mail.

Johnny was a farmer boy from Wathena, Kansas, a little fellow weighing barely one hundred pounds, but every inch a horseman. His reputation as a race rider was known up and down the Missouri — and Johnny was a showman. His bright red flannel shirt and blue trousers were almost hidden by a silver-spangled jacket and bat-wing chaps. A pair of holstered six-shooters hung at his hips, his rifle and horn were slung across his back, and silver spurs jangled at the heels of his fancy Spanish boots.

Sylph, the bay mare, was a beautiful Kentucky Thoroughbred, and Johnny had her rigged up like a parade horse, with massive silver-studded saddle and bridle. She pawed the ground nervously while Mr. Russell wrapped the packets of mail in waterproof silk and locked them into the four cantinas of the *mochila*. It was 7:15 when Mayor Thompson fired off a cannon and the race for San Francisco was officially on.

Johnny Frey had practiced well for this moment. As the crowd whistled, hooted, and cheered, he vaulted into his saddle without touching the stirrup. Rearing to her full height, the mare burst through the noisy crowd and raced down Jule Street toward the wharf. There the ferryboat waited to take them across the Missouri, to the little town of Elwood on the Kansas side of the river.

Showman that he was, Johnny Frey was first, last, and always a horseman. All the fancy trappings had been fine for the crowd in St. Joseph, but there was a race ahead — and a tough one. The minute he was on the ferry he pulled the

heavy trappings off the mare, and cinched on the lightweight Pony Express saddle. Next he shucked off his own fancy gear, including the rifle, and stowed it in a closet — where it would be handy for his return trip with the Pony Mail. On the trail he would give his horse the lightest load possible: buckskin shirt, breeches, and moccasins, his horn, and a pair of revolvers stuck under his belt.

The ferry had barely touched the Elwood landing when Johnny leaped the mare ashore and raced away into the darkening night. The Missouri Valley was then heavily wooded far to the westward, but Johnny Frey knew every trail through the timber as well as the deer and wolves that ran it.

Leaving Elwood, he turned the mare onto a winding trail that bore off along a creek to the southwest. As soon as they entered the timber the blackness closed in solidly. No man could have seen an arm's length, but horses can see in the dark much better than men. The mare threaded her way unerringly along the trail. From the feel of her body under him, Johnny read every twist and curve as well as if he could see. Where the branches were low, he lay close along the mare's neck, then, on the straightaways, urged her into her fastest pace.

Because the start had been more than two hours late, there was a lot of time to be made up if the Eastern riders were to equal or better the schedule set by Mr. Russell. And Johnny Frey was determined to make up his share of it. He drove the mare hard for the first ten miles, then ran a hand down along her neck — feeling for the heartbeat in the artery. It was strong and steady; no need to ease off yet.

Three miles out from Cold Springs Ranch, Johnny's first relay stop, the mare half stumbled — or did she falter? Quickly he slipped a hand beneath her flying mane, feeling for any nerve twitch that would tell of nearing exhaustion. He could feel none, but the mare was breathing hard now, and he knew her lungs must be burning. A little talking might take her mind off the pain. Stretched out along her neck with his face close to her unseen ears, he began soft-talking in rhythm with the beat of her hoofs,

"That's my girl, Sylphy. That's my pet. We'll show them Californy boys! We'll learn 'em what kind o' horsehair makes fiddle music!"

Carefully gauging the mare's remaining strength, Johnny held back just enough for a smart dash into the relay station. The keeper there had three beautiful daughters, and Johnny Frey liked to show off for pretty girls.

When at last Johnny rode out of the woods, a speck of light from the station twinkled across the prairie. Reaching for the horn, hung across his back, he blew three sharp blasts — the signal for the keeper to have a horse saddled and ready to go. A quarter-mile out, he called on the mare for her final sprint. With spurs just touching her flanks, and mouth close to her pinned-back ears, he whispered, "Now, girl! Now leave 'em hear the snare drum!"

Sylph responded like the Thoroughbred she was. Pouring out the last reserve of her strength, she quickened her pace until the sound of her hoofs rolled across the prairie like vibrant music. Then, sliding to a stop where the cheering keeper and his daughters waited with the relay horse, she stood with heaving sides and head hung to the ground.

The mare's hoofs were still sliding when Johnny leaped from the saddle, snatching up the *mochila* as he went. With a slap on her shoulder, he called, "Good horse, Sylph!" tossed the *mochila* over the saddle of the waiting pony, sprang aboard, and raced away.

Westward from the Cold Springs Ranch the prairies lay in rolling hills, with here and there a glimmer of light from some homesteader's soddy. There was no moon, but a few stars showed between the drifting clouds. Pushing the fresh pony as fast as he dared, Johnny headed out across the open prairies. Swerving a little now and again to skirt a creek bend or steep hill, he held a course straight for Kennekuk — 44 miles out of St. Joseph, and his next relay point.

Johnny's mount on that run was a strongly built Morgan, but it was winded and beginning to stagger when he brought it into Kennekuk. From there the route was easier for the ponies, but not too safe for the rider. It followed the old military road, veering off to the northwest, across the Kickapoo Indian Reservation, then on to Seneca, Kansas — 80 miles out from St. Joseph, and the end of Johnny's route.

Changing horses at Granada and Log Chain, Johnny Frey rode those last 36 miles in less than 2¾ hours. At 1:40 on the morning of April 4, he galloped his spent and dripping horse into the cheering crowd at the Seneca home station. In almost pitch-darkness he had ridden 80 miles in 6 hours and 25 minutes — nearly three times faster than the California mail had ever before been carried.

At the other end of the line, Jim Randall and his beautiful Palomino pony were still riding peacefully up the Sacramento River on the steamer *Antelope*.

3

THERE WAS NO wild celebration in Sacramento when, at 2:15 A.M. on April 4, Sam Hamilton and Bolivar Roberts — western superintendent for Russell, Majors & Waddell — stood in the darkness and rain, watching the steamer *Antelope* nose with annoying slowness toward its dock. For two days a steady drizzle had been falling, the streets were ankle-deep in mud, and riders splashing in from the foothills had reported a blizzard to be blowing in the high Sierra Nevada Mountains.

Bolivar Roberts was worried. The success or failure of the Pony Express might easily depend upon its first run. If the first mail were to be lost or fall far behind schedule, the whole venture might be ruined. And in deep mud no horse could run a 25-mile relay in the scheduled time. As soon as the rain began, he had sent word to have relay horses strung out at five- to eight-mile intervals along the trail. Each was to be kept saddled, blanketed, exercised, and grain-fed.

On the first report of a blizzard, Roberts had sent riders hurrying to the mountains with strings of pack mules. The mules were to be kept constantly on the move, treading out the trail through any canyons or passes where blowing snow was beginning to drift. Even if it took the pony rider a week to reach the summit, the mules must keep the trail open until he had passed.

Sam Hamilton, like the white mustang he held by the bridle reins, was mountain born and raised. And, like the mustang, he was not more than half tamed. He wore buckskins, with the hair left on to shed the rain. No rifle was slung across his back, but a pair of Colt .45's were shoved under his belt.

Sam's worry was because the *Antelope* was 2¼

hours late. He would carry the mail to Sportsman's Hall, 60 miles east of Sacramento and high in the foothills. From there, his friend, "Boston" Upson, had been chosen to make the rugged ride up and over the crest of the Sierras. With a blizzard blowing, Boston's chance of getting through with the mail was only one in ten, even in daylight. If night overtook him among the high peaks, his chance of living to get out was hardly one in a thousand. There was only one way for Sam to help his friend: he'd have to reach Sportsman's Hall by dawn, so that Boston could have every possible minute of daylight for his fight across the summit.

Jim Randall had tasted glory in San Francisco, and hoped for more at Sacramento. As the *Ante-*

lope neared its pier, he mounted his Palomino, ready to ride triumphantly down the gangplank. Sam Hamilton would have none of it. "Git off'n that nag!" he shouted. "Git that *mochila* to the rail and heave it here!"

Grabbing the *mochila* in mid-air, Sam slapped it across his saddle, and was on top of it before the rearing mustang got its hoofs back to the ground. His spurs raked from shoulder to flank as his feet found the stirrups, and the white mustang bolted away in a mud-splashing series of crowhops. With rein ends slashing, Sam raced up J Street, past the Capitol and Sutter's Fort, then eastward onto the Folsom road.

Seven miles out, there would be another mustang waiting, and this jug-headed white was tougher than sun-dried hickory. Seven miles through deep mud at top speed might kill him, but horseflesh was cheap compared to a friend's life — and every minute saved would give Boston a better chance.

Sam kept his spurs lashing and the line ends flailing for six miles. Then he felt the bronco beginning to weave in its stride. He'd have to

ease up a bit; better let the relay man at 7-Mile know he was coming. Pulling the horn over his shoulder, Sam blew three loud blasts. Panicked, the mustang tried to bolt out from under the sound, caught its stride, and galloped into the relay post with its last ounce of strength.

Hamilton wasted no time in telling the mustang it was a good horse. In one fast flow of motion, he jumped off the exhausted bronco with the *mochila* in his hands, flung it over the waiting pony's saddle, and leaped aboard. Without answering the "Good luck!" shouted after him, he spurred away toward the next relay post. The run to Folsom lay across the flat valley floor; here, if anywhere, time could be saved for Boston. There'd be no letting up on this mustang; he'd taste spurs all the way to 15-Mile House.

Sam's last horse into Folsom was a buckskin, with a black line down its back and zebra stripes on shoulders and forearms. Hamilton knew the horse and had ridden it many a time. There'd be no need for spurs and line ends now. This little bronco, if allowed, would run at top speed until he dropped dead in his tracks. The buckskin was within a minute of dropping when Sam slid him to a stop at the way station in Folsom.

That ride is one that will long stand in American horse history. On three half-wild mustangs, Sam Hamilton had ridden 20 miles through rain, mud, and darkness in 59 minutes. Few riders or horses could do it on dry ground in daylight.

From Folsom on there could be little hard galloping. The drizzle had become a steady rain, the night was pitch-dark, and the 27-mile run to Placerville was up and down steep hills and hogbacks. In the blackness, Sam had to let his mounts follow the trail as best they could, but he drove them to the limit of their endurance. Riding at top speed by feel alone, he must sense each slip or stumble in time to pull up the pony's head, help it regain its balance, and try to save it from a fall. Three times a horse went down before he could save it, but each time Sam jumped clear, and neither he nor the pony was badly injured. There was no dawn, but the blackness was thinning to murky gray as Sam spurred a mud-smeared mustang up the last long hill to Placerville.

From Placerville the trail wound steeply up Hangtown Gulch, rising more than 2000 feet in the 13-mile climb to Sportsman's Hall. As Sam spurred upward, the temperature fell and the rain turned into fine sleet, whipped down from the high mountains by a northeast wind. Ice-covered tree limbs crowded the trail, and the rocks underfoot became as slick as wet glass. Riding at any faster pace than a walk was treacherous, but Sam drove savagely. It was now light enough to see the trail — and every minute of daylight was one that Boston might need to save his life.

Midway to Sportsman's, a relay man waited with a fresh pony. A quarter-mile before reaching the spot, Sam's played-out mustang slipped, went down, and was unable to rise. In leaping from the saddle, Sam fell heavily, ripping his cheek against a boulder. Up in a moment, he blew four sharp blasts on his horn, snatched the *mochila* from his saddle, and ran toward the relay post. Alerted by the blasts, the relay man rode to meet him halfway, and within three minutes from the time his exhausted pony had fallen, Sam was driving ruthlessly up the trail.

Sam Hamilton was no man to pet or soft-talk a horse, but when Sportsman's Hall loomed through the grayness, he gave his drooping pony a slap on the shoulder. "Git along, old bronc," he said wearily. "Let's show 'em we ain't plumb wore down."

Lifting to a faltering, weaving gallop, the mustang pounded heavily up the trail to the Sportsman's Hall home station. The time was 6:18. In 4 hours and 3 minutes of rain-swept darkness, Sam Hamilton had ridden 60 miles, changed ponies eight times, and climbed nearly 4000 feet up the Sierra Nevadas.

Few words were spoken in the half-minute it took to swing the *mochila* over to Boston's saddle. He knew what Sam had been through, and why he had done it, but all he said was "Rough trip, Sam?"

" 'Twa'n't half bad," was the only answer. But as Boston's pony whirled and raced away, tough, untamed Sam Hamilton called, "*Vaya con Dios, Boston.*"

4

WHEN SAM HAMILTON had spurred ruthlessly through the night, no thought of racing against the Eastern riders had entered his mind. His only concern had been for Boston's safety. But, to the Midwestern riders, the race against the Californians and Mormons was on in earnest.

When Johnny Frey had galloped into Seneca and tossed the *mochila* to Jim Beatley, he had gained two hours on the schedule. Within half a minute, Jim was racing away to the west, determined to whittle off a couple of hours more.

Jim Beatley was in his middle thirties, but light and small. He was a Virginian, quick-tempered and hard-riding, but an excellent horseman. His route lay west along the road that is now U. S. Highway 36, then followed the Little Blue River northwest to Rock Creek — near the present town of Fairbury, Nebraska.

There was no moon, but the stars were bright, the road was good, and Jim had a fine Missouri race horse under him. He kept it at a swinging canter for the first 15 miles. Then, five miles short of Guittard's ranch, his first relay post, the horse began to falter in its stride. Jim felt quickly for a telltale nerve twitch in its neck, listened for a rasp in the sound of its breathing. Both were there. The horse was out of training and soft; another mile at that pace would break its wind and ruin it. Jim eased the horse to a walk, let it catch its wind, then went on at an easy lope.

The mount waiting for Jim at Guittard's was a Kentucky Thoroughbred. He knew the horse, had ridden her in a mile race at St. Joseph, and she had finished last. Already annoyed at the time lost by the softness of his first mount, Jim was furious at having drawn this worthless mare. In his anger, he galloped her hard for the first half mile, then slowed her to a swinging lope. With

25 miles to go, there was no sense in running her to death before he was fairly started. She'd give out all too soon anyway. Maybe he could pick up a decent horse in Marysville — if this one lasted that long.

Two miles passed, and three, and four — and the mare was still holding to that long-swinging, ground-covering lope. Jim ran a hand along her neck, listened for a rasp in her breathing. Everything seemed to be all right. The air whispered rhythmically through her nostrils, there was no nerve twitch, and her hide was hardly damp with sweat.

"Well, I'll be dogged!" Jim chuckled to himself. "No wonder this mare couldn't win a mile race; she's a distance runner, and a plumb good one if I don't miss my guess."

The mare was all that Jim had second-guessed her to be. There was no clattering of hoofs as she swung past the cheering crowd of early risers at Marysville. Her pace seemed slow, but its long-striding flow outdistanced the barking dogs that raced at her heels. Mile after mile the slim bay mare held her pace. And stride by stride, Jim

Beatley's admiration for her grew. Her breathing was still steady and even when the flicker of light from the Cottonwood relay station came into sight.

Jim was so far ahead of schedule that he knew the relay man would not yet be expecting him. As a warning to have a horse saddled and ready, he blew a loud blast on his horn. Startled at the sound, the mare leaped forward and sprinted the last mile as if she were fresh from the stable.

As Jim made a fast relay at Cottonwood, he shouted to the sleepy stableman, "Rub this mare down and cool her out slow; she's a plumb good one!" Then he spurred away in the starlight for the long run to his home station at Rock Creek.

Jim's third horse was strong and sturdy, but not fast. Although he drove hard, the sun was rising when he rode into the Rock Creek station and turned the mail over to "Doc" Brink.

Within ten seconds Doc had thrown the *mochila* over his own saddle and leaped aboard. Wheeling his rearing horse, he leaned from the saddle and said cautiously, "Wear your iron, and watch out for Dave McCanles, Jim! He's drunk

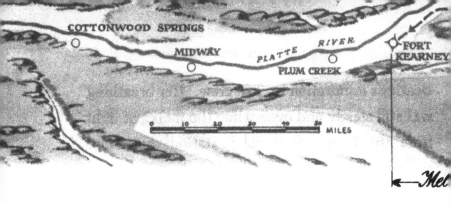

COTTONWOOD SPRINGS

MIDWAY

PLATTE RIVER

PLUM CREEK

FORT KEARNEY

0   10   20   30   40   50   MILES

—Mel

again and lookin' for a fight."

McCanles was a notorious bully and a fast man with a gun, but Jim Beatley had no fear of him. "You leave me do the worryin' about Dave McCanles," he told Doc. "You worry about gettin' that mail to Thirty-two-Mile! We're only three hours up on the schedule, and like as not, them boys west of the mountains are burnin' up the trail."

Doc Brink was in his early twenties. Though small, he was tough and strong, but almost childish in his love for fine horses. His route was the shortest and easiest of any pony rider's, barely 45 miles. With daylight and a change of mounts halfway, he might have gained a full hour on the schedule. Instead, he lost a half-hour by failing

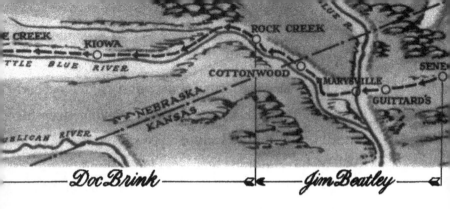

to drive either of his mounts nearly to the limit of its endurance. It was noon when he cantered up to the station at Thirty-two-Mile Creek and passed the *mochila* on to Melville Vaughn.

Mel Vaughn, thin and wiry, was a hardened frontiersman at twenty. All morning, he had been watching the sky to the west, and he didn't like the looks of it. A storm was closing in. Every possible minute must be gained before it struck, or the race with the Californians and Mormons might be lost. Heavy rain would turn the adobe soil of Platte River valley into soft mud, in which no horse could keep up to a nine-mile-an-hour schedule.

Mel didn't like the looks of Doc Brink's mount, either. One glance was enough to tell him that

the horse was far from spent, and that Doc had
been babying it. Slapping the *mochila* over his
saddle, he vaulted aboard with spurs raking.
What he shouted back at Doc came close to
breaking the pledge he had signed when he
became a Pony Express rider.

Mel's route was not an easy one. Leaving the
headwaters of Sandy Creek, the trail struck
northwest across a high, rolling divide — near the
present city of Hastings, Nebraska — then down
to Fort Kearney in the Platte River valley. With
only one change of horses in 60 miles, Mel drove
at the fastest pace he dared, but gained back only
20 minutes of the time Doc had lost. It was
twilight and beginning to rain when he galloped
his winded pony into Fort Kearney.

Over the Hump with Boston

BECAUSE TIME CHANGES as the Earth turns, it was two hours later in Nebraska than in California. So Doc Brink was well on his way when Sam Hamilton galloped up to Sportsman's Hall and turned the eastbound mail over to Warren Upson. But the name Upson does not appear on most lists of Pony Express riders. In its place one finds "Boston," nickname for the five-foot, twenty-year-old boy who carried the first Pony Mail over the big hump of the Sierra Nevadas.

Boston was the son of a wealthy California publisher, but from earliest childhood his only interest had been in horses and mountains. He loved them both, and understood their every mood and trick. He could tame the wildest bronco, knew the Sierras as well as Kit Carson knew the Rockies, and had ridden trails that only he and the Indians had ever seen.

Sam Hamilton's fear had been that night would overtake Boston among the high peaks. Boston himself knew there would be no possible chance of getting through unless he reached the summit before three o'clock. With a northeast gale blowing, there would be twenty- to thirty-foot snowdrifts on the high range by late afternoon, and mule trains would be unable to keep the trail open.

The first five miles of Boston's route lay along a heavily timbered divide, rising ruggedly to the south rim of the American River Gorge. Then, for six miles, the trail pitched steeply down a rocky mountainside to the river — a drop of nearly a thousand feet. Until he reached the rim, Boston kept his pony at a pounding trot, sparing it only on the steepest rises. That gait would shake a man's liver loose, but it was the safest and fastest way to travel an icy trail. A galloping horse would tire faster, and was twice as apt to slip, fall, and break a leg.

Where the trail pitched down to the river, Boston dismounted and drove the pony before him. Carrying a rider's weight, a tired pony couldn't possibly keep its footing on the sleet-covered rocks; but riderless, a mountain mustang could slide like an expert skier. Slipping, sliding, catching their balance against trees, and plunging on, Boston and the pony slithered to the bottom of the gorge.

No more than a brook in dry times, the south fork of the American River was in flood. Sixty feet wide at the ford, and littered with deadwood, it swirled through the S-shaped gorge like a great snake writhing in anger. After studying the racing water for a minute or two, Boston took the *mochila* from his saddle, tossed it around his shoulders and mounted. He rode upstream for 40 yards, then carefully poised the pony on a ledge at the river's brink. Watching for a clear stretch of water between the deadwood, he drove his spurs hard, at the same moment swinging the *mochila* above his head.

At the strike of Boston's spurs, the mustang

leaped far out over the swirling water, dropped, and went under in a geyser of splashing foam. In an instant its head bobbed to the surface, and it struck out for the far bank, driving with all the strength of its sturdy legs. Boston had judged the current well: the pony's hoofs hit bottom right where the trail dipped down to the ford, and it scrambled, dripping, up the bank.

Boston was soaked to the armpits, but the mail was still dry. Knowing he would be in for a wetting, he had made preparations for it. In a cedar grove just beyond the river, he had a relay man waiting with a fresh pony, a roaring fire, and dry clothing. Within three minutes from the time he had come out of the river, Boston had changed clothing and was again riding rapidly up the trail.

From the ford the trail followed the north side of the river to its source at the foot of the high western rampart of the Sierras. Only a few feet above the angry river at some places, but more than 1000 at others, the trail twisted and wound upward, clinging to the steep mountainsides. Halfway up lay Hope Valley, given its name because there was hope for any blizzard-bound traveler who succeeded in getting that far out of the high mountains. For a man going in, it might well have been named Hopeless.

Early April blizzards were not uncommon in the high mountains, but Boston had never known one to be this cold. Sweeping across the snow-fields at the summit of the range, the wind raced down through the V-shaped funnel of the gorge in a freezing blast. He bent his head against it and kept his pony at a trot wherever the trail was not too steep.

Snow was beginning to drift around the Hope Valley relay station when Boston plodded up on his exhausted pony. His muscles were already stiffening with the cold, but he would not stop to thaw them out or to eat. Hard as he had driven, it had taken 2½ hours to make the 20-mile ride from Sportsman's Hall. Gulping a cup of steaming coffee, he slipped the *mochila* onto his next mount, and was away up the trail within two minutes.

Above Hope Valley the gorge narrowed, the drop-off to the river became nearly straight down, and the trail climbed steeply along the canyon wall. Two miles out, fine blowing snow closed in like smothering powder, blotting out the chasm to Boston's right and the towering mountainside at his left. The drifts began to deepen, and low-bent saplings often blocked the trail.

Two miles an hour was considered fair time for a pack train over this part of the trail in good weather. Boston was determined to travel at better than twice that speed. Out of the saddle nearly as much as in it, he helped his pony along by climbing afoot where the trail was the steepest.

plowing ahead through drifts, and hunting out the quickest and safest way around the blockades. Boston carried no watch, but had a mountain man's inborn sense of time, and drove himself and his pony ruthlessly to hold to the pace he had set.

On the high headlands, close to the chasm rim, the gale swept the trail clear of snow, threatening to sweep Boston and his pony with it. In the lee of the mountain shoulders the drifts piled higher with each succeeding mile. Before reaching the next relay station they had plowed

through a dozen shoulder-high drifts, and were forced to make three treacherous detours around blockades. Even so, the first six miles up from Hope Valley were made in an hour and ten minutes.

The change of mounts took only the two minutes allowed by regulations, but between swallows of hot coffee, Boston asked, "What happened to the mule trains, Pete? Didn't see a sign of 'em."

"All up toward the summit," the stationkeeper answered. "Snow's a-blowin' terrible up there — drifts nigh on to thirty foot deep. Don't you go tryin' to get through alone, Boston! You get behind a mule train, so's it can break fresh trail for you."

"Don't you worry, Pete, I'll make out," was all Boston said as he climbed into the saddle and headed back into the storm.

The five miles to Strawberry, the next relay post, were much like the six before them, except that the drifts were deeper, and the temperature dropped with every rise of the trail. Boston had to begin saving his own strength for the upper rampart, but was determined to hold a four-mile pace. Without his help the pony tired rapidly. It was barely able to drag itself through the drifts on the last half-mile climb to Strawberry. Still, nothing had been seen of the mule trains.

All the stationkeeper could tell Boston was, "Ain't saw hide nor hair of 'em, but Yancy's supposed to be bustin' trail twixt here and Yank's. You'd best wait up, Boston! If Yancy can't make it with six mules, you ain't got a chance with that little cayuse."

Boston knew the man might be right, but as he swung onto a waiting pony, he shouted above the howl of the wind, "Keep that coffee hot, Charlie! Reckon I know where Yancy is, and he'll need it when he gets out." Then he spurred away into the whiteness of the storm.

Two miles above Strawberry, Boston found Yancy and his mules — right where he expected to find them. Here the trail skirted a solid-rock mountain shoulder, dipping in around a deep pocket. The wind had swept the shoulder naked, forming a whirlwind in the pocket and dropping a thirty-foot drift of feathery snow. Yancy had driven his mules back and forth across the drift all morning, trying to keep a solid trail packed. Then, halfway across, the lead mule had stepped off into soft snow, broken a leg and fallen back across the trail, blocking it completely. Yancy had been lucky to get himself and the rest of the mules out before they were buried alive.

Any other man than Boston would have been turned back, but he had found that pocket blocked before, and had discovered a way around it. Backtracking a short distance, he dismounted and led his pony onto a narrow shelf that wound steeply up the rock face of the mountain. The footing was hardly fit for a mountain goat, but step by slow step Boston worked his way up the ledge, and his pony followed. Circling the pocket many feet above the blocked trail, they clung to the canyon wall like lizards, with the wind threatening to tear them loose at every cautious step.

The climb was dangerous enough, but getting back down to the trail was far worse. The backlash of the wind whipped snow into their faces as if shot from a cannon. Blanketing the smooth rock, the light snow gave no footing, and Boston

had to try each foothold carefully before he dared put his weight on it. One misstep would hurl him to the bottom of the gorge in an avalanche.

Yancy, unable to be of any help, watched breathlessly as Boston worked his way cautiously down the canyon side. "You'll never make it through, kid," he shouted as Boston led his trembling pony back onto the trail. "Better hole up till this blow is over and they get enough mules in here to open up the trail."

"Shucks, this is nothing," Boston shouted back. "You should see a January howler up here! Try to get that drift open, Yancy; I'll be back with the St. Joe mail in a week. See you later. *Hasta la vista!*" Then he was back in the saddle and fighting his way up the trail, head bent to the wind and arms thrashing to warm his blood.

For one of the first times in his life, Boston lost all track of time in his fight to the top of the summit. He was unable to see more than a few feet ahead, and had to be afoot most of the time: helping his pony through drifts, feeling his way along precipice edges, and clambering up the steepest grades.

The mule drivers had done their job as well as they could. They had kept three of the worst drifts passable, but had been unable to tramp out the rest of the trail as fast as the snow blew in. Time and again Boston had to pick his way along a mountainside to get past a blockade. Twice, after he reached the head of the river gorge, he became completely lost in the veering, shifting winds that swept around the high peaks. Only his knowledge of the mountains and his pony's instinct saved their lives.

In one of his forced detours Boston missed his last relay post on the western rampart. When he realized he was beyond it, it was too late to turn back. There was nothing to do but to help his already tired-out pony as much as he could and push on. Weariness such as he had never known dragged at him in the thin air. Each foot seemed to be weighted with lead, and the drowsiness of cold and exhaustion numbed his brain. To fight off the drowsiness he flailed his arms and slapped his face sharply, stirring the blood and driving it to his sleepy brain.

From the pitch of the trail, Boston knew he was within a half mile of the summit when his pony floundered in a snowbank, fell, and was unable to rise. Hauling the *mochila* from the saddle, he threw it over his shoulders and staggered, almost drunkenly, up the last steep grade to the relay station at the summit of the Sierras.

"You're plumb beat out, kid," the keeper told him. "You stay here with me till this storm passes. Trailhead on the east side's twenty foot under snow — blocked solid. There couldn't no man get past nor through it."

"Thanks, Jim," Boston answered, "but I'm going to make a try at it. If I can't get past I'll be back. While you can still follow the tracks I left, you might make a try at getting that pony of mine out of the snowbank. He's too good a horse to let freeze."

With the wind from the northeast, the far shoulder of the summit was the trickiest spot on the crossing. There the trail turned to the north, angling sharply down the face of a bald stone mountain, with a thousand-foot drop-off to a timber-lined gorge at the right. There was no possibility of circling above the blockade, but Boston thought he could get past in the gorge below. He remembered having once seen a game trail that wound through the timber there, high along the canyon side. If he could find it now and find his way back to the regular trail at the other end, the rest of the trip shouldn't be too hard.

Just east of the summit Boston turned his fresh pony off the trail and plunged it down over the rim of the gorge. Here the drop-off was not so steep as farther on, and, not too far down, there was an aspen thicket to catch them if they tumbled. Squatting on its haunches, the pony kept right side up until they hit the aspen thicket. Then, bumping from tree to tree, it lost its balance

and somersaulted, throwing Boston head over
heels.

It was a lucky fall. When Boston picked himself up, he found the tree trunks around him

scarred with blackened lines. He knew them to be the markings left by deer and elk when scraping the spring fuzz from their antlers, so the trail must be close by. Remounting and following the thickest markings, he had no trouble in finding the trail he remembered. And, as game trails always do, it followed the easiest route along the gorge side. Covered by thick timber, it was protected from the wind, and blown snow sifted down gently through the trees.

Boston had followed the game trail at a good pace for about two miles, when it left the heavy timber and came out into another aspen thicket. He recognized the grove in a moment. It lay just below the regular mule trail, halfway down the steep pitch from the summit. Quickly climbing to the trail above, he was surprised to find the snow barely knee-deep and not badly drifted. Here the force of the wind was far less than on the western side of the summit, and there was much less flying snow.

A mile farther down the trail, Boston rode out from under the storm. The air cleared, and in the great basin below him Lake Tahoe lay like a gigantic blue mirror, more than a mile above sea level and surrounded by a high wall of jagged, snow-capped mountains.

Through the murk overhead, the disk of the sun shone dimly. Boston stared up at it in disbelief. It seemed a thousand hours since he had ridden out of the relay station at Hope Valley, but the sun was only about two hours past mid-sky. With only a few inches of snow on the ground, he put his pony down the last dip of the trail at a pounding trot, then galloped it across the valley. Ten miles ahead, where the California-Nevada line crosses Lake Tahoe, was Friday's Station, the end of his route.

It was 2:18 when Boston galloped his pony up to Friday's Station and turned the mail over to "Pony Bob" Haslam. In a howling storm that few men could have lived through, he had carried the first Pony Mail 55 miles across the high hump of the Sierra Nevadas in just 8 hours — much better time than the schedule called for in summer weather.

6

TWENTY YEARS OLD, weighing barely a hundred pounds, and as tough as spring steel, "Pony Bob" Haslam was known all through the desert country as "The Ridin' Fool." Pony Bob was one of the most daring horsemen who ever lived — hard-riding, hard-fighting, and sometimes seemingly reckless, but he was no fool. And he was out to show "them Eastern dudes," that they were really in a race.

A mile beyond Friday's Station, Bob turned his galloping mustang sharply from the lake, up a long sand dune, and into the mouth of a rough canyon. There he jerked the six-shooter from his belt, cocked it, and held it ready for action. The

Paiute Indians had been threatening to go on the warpath for months, and this was one of their favorite ambush places.

Narrowing and becoming more rugged, the canyon snaked steeply up through pinnacled out-croppings of sandstone and enormous boulders — every one of them an ideal hiding place for an Indian on the warpath. Speed was the best defense against flying arrows in that narrow canyon, and Pony Bob had speed to spare. The mountain mustang he rode was less than half broken, spur-shy, and tougher than rawhide. The day before, it had taken five strong men to hog-tie it and nail on its first shoes. The steep three-mile run up to Daggett's Pass would do it no harm. To make the poorest possible target, Pony Bob lay tight against the bronco's neck — and he wasn't too careful with his spurs.

Horse and rider came through the pass at the head of the canyon in a blur of speed. Quickly Bob hauled the wild-eyed mustang into a tight circle to stop its runaway dash. Even this moun-tain-born mustang would break its neck if it hit the drop-off too fast.

Daggett's Pass stands at the top of the western mountain wall that rims the Nevada deserts. Steeper than a cathedral roof, the wall drops off more than 2000 feet to the Carson River marshes at its base. A mule trail wound down the mountainside in a series of long loops, but Pony Bob didn't bother with the trail. He had picked and shod this particular mustang for only two reasons: it was afraid of nothing, and could slither down steep mountains without losing its balance.

At the edge of the descent, Bob shoved the gun back into his belt, hauled his saddle cinch tight, pulled his hat snug, and touched the bronco's flanks with his spurs. Leaping forward, the mustang plunged over the rim, landing in a half-squat — hind feet spread wide, forelegs set like bracing poles, and tail hugging the mountainside as a rudder.

Skating, sliding, bouncing aside to avoid boulders and bushes, the bronco streaked down the mountain in an avalanche of broken brush, snow, and rolling stones. With every muscle set for a quick leap, Bob threw his body from side to side: anticipating the mustang's moves, going with them, and helping it keep its balance.

By the trail, it was six miles to the foot of the mountain. The way Bob and his pony went, it was little more than a mile, and couldn't have taken over two minutes. The excited, half-wild bronco hit the flat land at the mountain base in a series of bounding leaps, bogged its head, and went into a fit of bucking. Happy, and screeching like an Indian full of firewater, Pony Bob rode out the buck with spurs raking and hat fanning. Then, turning to the north along the river edge, he raced the still eager mustang for the relay stop at Genoa — the old Mormon Station, first white settlement in Nevada.

Every mount in Bob Haslam's string was a half-wild bronco. A desert man, he had picked himself a string of mustangs that could match the desert's cruelty with speed and endurance. The 12-mile trail to Carson City lay snowless and almost level. Up on another bronco at Genoa, Bob drove at top speed for the full distance. He carried neither rifle nor horn; he wouldn't be bothered with them. As he raced into town he raised a war whoop that could have been heard

at the top of the mountains.

Carson City was then a city in name only. Less than two years old, it was the supply town for the mines of the Comstock Lode. Its one street was little more than a double row of saloons, a few assay offices, a general store, and the hotel that was the relay station. At the sound of Pony Bob's whoop, a crowd of miners gathered in front of the hotel, yelling and cheering. They scattered like frightened chickens as Bob raced his foam-spattered bronco straight at them. It was sliding to a stop when he flipped out of the saddle, bringing the *mochila* with him. Another flip and he was up and away on a fresh mustang, racing for Dayton, his next relay post, 11 miles to the northeast. Five miles beyond Dayton he turned sharply to the east, following Carson River through a notch in a low mountain chain.

Beyond the notch the river spread out into a wide swamp, rimmed with bush and aspen and lying between barren desert hills. This was another favorite Indian ambush spot. Safety demanded that a rider stay at least a gunshot away from the swamp, high along the rough hillsides. No one knew the danger better than Pony Bob, but he held his course tight along the hard ground at the swamp edge. In this way he could cut the distance from Carson City to Fort Churchill to 35 miles and save at least 30 minutes. Lying flat on the neck of a racing pony, he was a poor target for arrows, and the Nevada Indians had few good rifles.

Pony Bob paid no attention to pacing his mounts as he rode. Born wild, descendants of Spanish war horses, these desert mustangs could carry a light rider at top speed for an hour or more. On this first trip with the mail Bob had no relay that long, so he drove for every ounce of speed in his horses' legs, cutting the scheduled time by nearly two-thirds.

At Reed's, ten miles downriver from Dayton, Pony Bob changed mounts in 20 seconds, and dashed away on the last 15-mile stretch of his route. The hands of the clock in the thick-walled adobe station at Fort Churchill stood at 5:35 when he streaked in and tossed the *mochila* to Bart Riles, the next Pony rider.

In 15 hours and 20 minutes, three determined riders — hardly more than boys — had carried the first Pony Express mail 185 of the most rugged miles on the entire route to St. Joseph. Only Pony Bob had thought of his ride as a race against the riders east of the Rockies, but they had made up the time lost by the *Antelope* and had gained more than nine hours on the schedule set up by Mr. Russell.

The Prairie Riders

7

Because of the two-hour difference in time between the Midwest and West, Pony Bob was just making his relay in Carson City when Mel Vaughn galloped his winded pony into Fort Kearney.

Rough as Mel had been with Doc Brink for babying his horses, he cautioned Billie Campbell as he tossed him the *mochila,* "Take it easy now, Billie! We're nigh on to three hours ahead of schedule a'ready. If this rain keeps up it'll be blacker'n tar out there, and there'll be knee-deep mud 'fore daylight. Don't run no risk of stirrin' up a stampede or playin' a horse out and gettin' left afoot amongst them wolves and Injuns!"

There was good reason for Mel's cautioning. Billie was just past eighteen, his 100-mile route lay in the Platte River valley, and the only white men were those at the relay stations, 25 miles apart. Elsewhere the Indians roamed and wolves howled around the drifting buffalo herds.

Regardless of Mel's warning, Billie had no intention of taking it easy. There was no telling how fast those riders west of the Rockies might be burning up the trail, and he didn't plan to lie back and let them steal the race. Murky twilight lasted for nearly an hour after he left Fort Kearney, and he made the most of it. Keeping clear of the deep-rutted Oregon Trail, he headed straight westward at a smart gallop. By the time black darkness fell he was halfway to his first relay station. Though he could see nothing himself, he knew from the sound of his horse's hoofs that it had returned to the trail and was following it. He pushed on at a brisk canter, and had cut 15 minutes from the schedule when he reached his first relay.

Although wet and cold, Billie was in high spirits when he rode into Midway, his second relay station. In spite of the darkness and rain, he had gained another 15 minutes, and the longest half of his route was behind him. His last mount had been one of the finest horses he had ever ridden. It was a sturdy, willing and intelligent Morgan. Countless wolves had howled in the blackness around them, but the horse had shown no fear, sticking to the trail in a steady, ground-covering lope.

Billie's third mount was a fine-boned, high-headed Kentucky gelding. It reared and plunged when the *mochila* was thrown across its saddle, trying to break away and bolt back to the stable. Billie had seen plenty of home-run prairie horses and knew how to handle them: a good spurring would get the stable out of their minds in a hurry. Excellent rider and plainsman that he was, he knew nothing about highstrung racing horses. He leaped onto the unruly gelding's back, lashing with his spurs as he landed.

Billie couldn't have made a worse mistake. The horse, unused to the wild country and already frightened, was thrown into a panic. The keeper should have known better than to send the horse out on such a night, but he shouted, "That's the stuff, Billie! Give the crazy outlaw a taste o' iron! Learn him who's the boss!"

It took Billie Campbell only a few minutes to realize his mistake: this gelding was no outlaw; it was a good horse, only young and panicked by fright. Billie tried to soothe and quiet it, but he was too late. The horse was now as afraid of the man on its back as of the wolves that howled in the darkness.

Guiding himself by the speck of light from the station, and holding his mount to a dancing, side-stepping walk, Billie tried to line him out on the westbound trail. When the horse had quieted a little, Billie let him lope slowly, weaving him back and forth only enough to find and keep near the trail.

For an hour the system worked well. At a lope, the gelding was less nervous, and each time he struck the trail he followed it a little better. Then, suddenly and from nearby, a wolf howled. Rearing, whirling and plunging at the sound, the frightened horse raced away through the blackness at breakneck speed. The Platte River, filled

with quicksand, could be no more than a half
mile away, and Billie couldn't tell whether his
mount was racing toward or away from it. He
could only haul on the reins, pull the gelding's
head to one side, and try to turn him in a circle.

The leverage of a curb bit on a horse's mouth
is powerful and painful, but the gelding was
panicked beyond the feeling of pain. Pull as he
might, Billie couldn't bring the frightened runaway under control. His only comfort was that
the horse must be running away from the river.
If not, he would already have plunged into it.

Billie's first fear was just passing when a worse
one overtook him. From ahead and at both sides
he heard the sound of loud grunting. He knew
it for the sound that sleeping buffaloes made
when wakened and lunging to their feet. Short,
angry bellows came from the darkness, then the
pounding of a thousand racing hoofs.

Billie nearly lost his seat as the gelding
checked, wheeled, and raced again. Within
seconds they were in the midst of a roaring river
of stampeding buffaloes. This was no time for
gentle handling of the panicked gelding, and

there was no use in trying to guide it with the reins. Billie grabbed the saddle horn with both hands, swung a boot high, and spurred hard on the neck and shoulder — forcing his horse away from the loudest roar, the center of the stampeding herd.

Battered from side to side, they were swept along like driftwood in a torrent, but the gelding managed to keep its feet. It seemed hours before the thunder of pounding hoofs became less deaf-

ening and only stragglers raced around them. Still spurring, Billie drove the gelding outward until they were clear of the stragglers, then turned him in a tight circle and brought him to a stop. With the danger passed, his own nerves cracked for a minute. There in the blackness and rain, both horse and rider stood trembling as if they had Saint Vitus's dance.

Billie Campbell was no man to let his nerves get the best of him for long. Fortunately, the

mail was still safe, and it was his job to get it to Cottonwood Springs as fast as he could. While he tried to decide which way to go, the reins pulled in his hand; the horse had raised its head and was looking around. It turned, took a few walking steps, then settled into a straightaway trot. That was enough for Billie. The horse had found his bearings and was heading for the stable — the only safety it knew. If it was as smart as he thought, it would go to the Oregon Trail and try to follow this back to Midway.

Billie left the reins loose, letting the horse choose its own direction and speed. Shortly it moved into a lope, then a brisk canter, but held straight on. After three or four miles, Billie heard the splash of soft mud underfoot. He knew they were on the trail, and felt sure they were headed east. A moment later he knew he was right. The gelding fought the reins when he turned it around and forced it to go the other way.

Soaked from head to foot, and shivering in the cold rain, Billie fought the gelding westward hour after hour. It would not hold to the trail, kept trying to turn back, and had to be reined constantly. Six or seven times a wolf howl sent it off in a runaway panic. Each time Billie had to spur it into circling, let it find the homeward trail, then turn it back to the west. Gray dawn was breaking when he rode the worn-out gelding into his third relay station at Willow Island.

The keeper offered to take the *mochila* on to the next station, but Billie wouldn't let him. "Thank you kindly," he said, "but I'm gettin' paid to carry the mail clean through to Cottonwood Springs, and I aim to do it without help. I a'ready lost a heap of time, but in daylight I reckon I can make some of it up." Stopping only to gulp a cup of hot coffee, he swung onto his next horse and loped away.

Even in daylight, Billie couldn't hold to the schedule. The nightlong rain had soaked the Platte River valley until a horse's hoofs cut in to the pasterns. Although his mount was a good one, Billie was more than three hours in riding the last relay of his route. He had done the best he could, but had lost five hours on the schedule — the three the others had gained, and two besides.

Dead tired from 16 hours in the saddle, Billie

Campbell could still joke when he rode into Cottonwood Springs. As Little Yank snatched the *mochila* and threw it across his saddle, he snapped, "You're two hours late, kid! That's no way to win races!"

"I'm plumb sorry, Yank," Billie told him, "but they give me a homin' pigeon 'stead of a horse to ride out of Midway."

As Little Yank wheeled his horse away, he called back, "Never mind, Billie boy, I'll make it up again 'fore I hit Julesburg."

"If you do, you'll need one of them horses with wings," Billie shouted after him.

Little Yank had ridden less than a mile before he realized how right Billie had been. His route lay for 100 miles along the South Platte River,

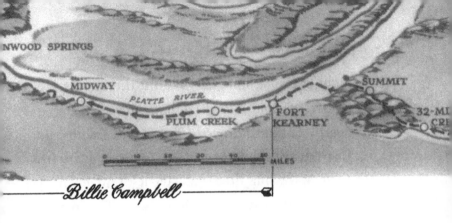

and the valley was a sea of mud. Although he was mounted on a fast Thoroughbred, the heavy muck dragged at its hoofs, holding it back and sapping its strength. The best pace it could hold was a back-wrenching trot.

Hour after hour the rain fell steadily, the mud grew deeper, and Little Yank grew more disgusted. Each of his first three mounts had been brought from Kentucky, and they were not yet accustomed to the wild country. The buffalo herds, and the wolves that howled in the distance, frightened them into wasting their strength in useless plunging. Yank was unable to judge their endurance, and either tired them too soon or failed to get the best out of them.

Long before he reached his third relay station,

night overtook him, and with it the wolves grew bolder. Their blood-chilling howls from the nearby darkness drove his horse into a wild panic. Rearing and plunging, it tried to race away from each howl, but tired quickly in the deep mud and could make little headway. The nerves under its hide began to quiver, and Yank knew it was nearing exhaustion. The wolves knew it too, and closed in for the kill.

Little Yank emptied a revolver into the blackness, but the shots frightened his mount more than they frightened the wolves. He had barely brought the horse back under control when the pack was again at its heels. Yank didn't dare empty the second gun. In desperation, he snatched his horn over his shoulder and blew it with all his might. Startled yipes came from the darkness as the wolves drew back in fear.

For two hours, Yank held the wolves off with his horn, while his exhausted mount dragged on at a plodding walk. When at last they reached the relay station at Diamond Springs, the horse stood with its head hanging to the ground — completely ruined.

With darkness, a wind had sprung up. By the time Little Yank rode out of Diamond Springs it had risen to a gale from the northwest, whipping the rain before it. At any other time he would have hated to ride in such a storm, but that night it was a blessing. From it he could tell his direction without following the Oregon Trail, and it drove the wolves to cover.

Riding straight south across the drenched valley, Little Yank followed a winding gulch up onto the rolling hills of the high prairie, then turned so that the rain struck full against his right cheek. Julesburg, Colorado, the end of his route, would lie straight ahead. And up here on the hills the thick-matted buffalo grass gave his horse good footing.

Yank rode at a steady lope, slowing his horse only through hollows where buffaloes might be huddled away from the storm. His last 25-mile ride was by far his fastest and easiest, but it was nearly midnight when he forded the South Platte River and rode into Julesburg. Instead of making up any of Billie Campbell's time, he had lost another five hours — and it was only through an oversight that he had not lost six. When Mr. Russell had laid out the Pony Express route schedules, he had made no allowance for the fact that a traveler must set his watch ahead or back one hour whenever he crosses a time zone boundary line. Yank had started his ride in the Central Time Zone, and had gained an hour when, near his first relay station, he rode into the Mountain Time Zone. Even so, the mail had fallen seven hours behind schedule, and the race with the California and Mormon riders seemed as good as lost.

8

BILLIE CAMPBELL was already nearing his first relay station when Pony Bob Haslam streaked into Fort Churchill and flung the eastbound *mochila* to Bart Riles. In Nebraska it was pitch-dark, but on the Nevada deserts it was still full daylight.

Bart was a thin, quiet Mexican boy. He spoke almost no English, but was an excellent horseman and knew the Nevada deserts and mountains as no other except the Indians knew them. On the darkest night he could find his way unerringly across the trackless wilderness. It was for this reason that he had been chosen to carry the mail east from Fort Churchill. With Paiute Indian trouble brewing, his 117-mile route to Smith's Creek was the most treacherous on the entire Pony Express trail.

Bart had not understood the pledge he was taking when he made an X behind his name and became a Pony Express rider. But he understood Pony Bob's *"Guarde con su vida, y darle prisa, amigo!"* (Guard it with your life, and hurry, friend!) Pony Bob was Bart's hero. Although Bart was inclined to be timid, there was no hardship or danger he wouldn't face to please Bob and win his praise. He raced his pony out of the fort as if Satan were at his heels.

One sometimes thinks of the desert as a great expanse of barren, shifting sand, but the Nevada desert is quite different. It is broken by almost a hundred separate mountain chains, all running north and south, and the arid stretches between are dotted with sagebrush and greasewood. Its few rivers have no outlets to the sea, but spread into great marshes before being swallowed by the thirsty soil. Nearly 500 miles of the Pony Express route lay through this desolate and uninhabited wilderness.

Bart's first relay station was at the end of the Carson River Marsh, 30 miles east of Fort Churchill. To save a long ride around, the Pony Express trail had been hacked through the willow and aspen thickets that dotted the swamp. In daylight these were ideal Indian ambushes. At night a rider on a racing horse gave the Indians no target, but the swamp was far from safe. It was the favorite hunting ground of lynx and cougar, and for miles the trail twisted through bogs so deep that they had to be matted with willow saplings. If a running pony missed a turn it would be mired and the rider thrown. If not killed, he was an easy prey for Indians or wild animals.

The sky was a sullen gray when Bart put his pony onto the marsh trail. Flattened down to give the least possible target for bullets or arrows, he threaded the winding pathway at reckless speed for the remaining hour of daylight. Then the night settled, black and starless. Over the treacherous bogs Bart had to hold his pony to a walk, and there the mosquitoes swarmed in millions. They drove the pony frantic, and cov-

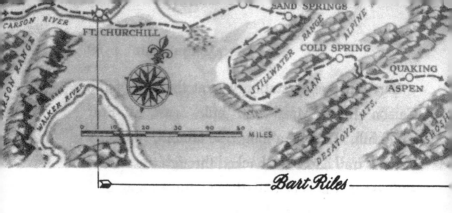

ered Bart's face in a stinging, bloodsucking mass.

Bart's face was so swollen that he was hardly recognizable when, after three hours, he reached the Stillwater relay post. To keep his eyes from closing completely, he smeared his face with grease, then flipped onto his remount and galloped away. On a starlit night he could ride the 20 miles to Sand Springs in an hour and a half, but in the blackness it took an hour longer. It was just midnight when he rode in, made a fast relay, and headed out for Cold Spring — 37 miles to the east, and across the Stillwater and Clan Alpine mountain ranges.

Bart was less than a half-hour out of Sand Springs when he spied three or four specks of light, glimmering starlike through the blackness

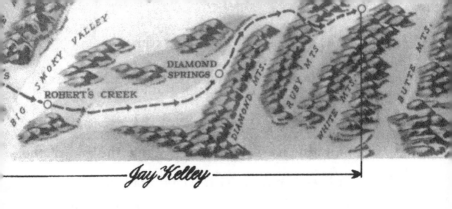

ahead. A few minutes later the hoot of an owl came from the darkness behind him. Then, as if echoed back by the mountains, it came faintly from far ahead and above. Bart stopped his pony and sat watching and listening. That was no owl hoot, and those specks of light were not stars. Again the echo came, more faintly and from higher on the mountains. Then, one by one, the specks of light disappeared.

Carefully Bart turned his pony off the trail, riding southward at a noiseless jog. Those specks of light had been from Indian campfires at the pass across the summit. The owl hoots were signals, telling of his coming. In starlight, he would have risked running the ambush, but in the black darkness it would be foolhardy. In that narrow pass he would be trapped like a rat in a hole.

There was only one way to get past the ambush: he would have to circle the end of the Stillwater range. That would double the length of his ride and, in black darkness, would be tricky business. For an hour Bart rode in absolute silence, guiding himself by coyote howls that came now and again from behind and above him. These too were Indian signals, passing the word that he had left the trail and escaped.

When he could no longer hear the howls, Bart stopped his pony and raised a coyote howl of his own, then listened for the direction and timing of the echo. Using the mountains as a sounding board, and guiding himself by the echo, Bart rode as fast as his pony could pick its way in the darkness. At dawn he had rounded the end of the range, but was 18 miles farther from Cold Spring than he had been at Sand Springs. Cutting straight eastward, he crossed the Clan Alpine range at its lower end, then made the 40-mile waterless run to Cold Spring. It was midafternoon when he rode in on his completely spent pony.

While Bart wolfed down beans and biscuits Jim McNaughton, the keeper, warned him in a mixture of Spanish and English: during the night the Desatoya Mountains had been speckled with Indian fires. The pass was sure to be ambushed. He must run no risk of being caught by the Indians and losing the mail.

The keeper was still talking when Bart mounted and rode away. He had understood enough; with daylight and his knowledge of the mountains, he was sure he could get past the ambush. The Indians couldn't be everywhere; if they were watching the regular pass he knew others that would be unguarded. There was only one spot on the 30-mile trail to Smith's Creek that worried him. That was Quaking Aspen Bottom, between the Desatoya and Shoshone Mountains. There the Pony Express trail had been cut through a two-mile aspen thicket, and there was no way around it.

Circling danger spots and threading his way upward through rugged canyons, Bart crossed the backbone of the Desatoyas, then cautiously slipped back to the trail near Quaking Aspen

Bottom. After resting his pony, he raced through the thicket amid war whoops and flying arrows, but came out untouched. It was past two o'clock in the afternoon when he reached Smith's Creek. Few men, if any, could have matched Bart's ride, but it had taken over 20 hours — three more than the schedule allowed.

Jay Kelley, though jockey-size, was among the greatest of the desert riders, but he lacked Bart's uncanny ability to find his way through black darkness. Storm clouds blanketed the sky when he took the *mochila* from Bart and galloped away on his 116-mile route to Ruby Valley.

Without sun the desert afternoon was cool, and Jay had little need to spare his ponies. Like Bart, he had to avoid several Indian ambushes, but had few mountains to cross, and had covered 50 miles of his route by twilight. He was gloating over the pace he was setting for "them Eastern braggers," when his troubles began. The night fell dead black, his pony wouldn't follow the faint trail, and Jay lost half the night in blind wandering over the desert. Twice, after daylight, he had to race for his life to get away from well-mounted warriors, and it was nine in the morning before he rode into Ruby Valley Station. He had not only lost all the advantage gained by his fast riding of the afternoon, but had fallen two hours behind the time established for his route.

The Foothill Riders

9

Wʜɪʟᴇ Jᴀʏ Kᴇʟʟᴇʏ was wandering blindly on the Nevada deserts, "Joyous Jack" Keetley was taking the westbound *mochila* from Little Yank at Julesburg, Colorado, in a driving rainstorm.

Jack was one of the best known and best liked of all the Pony Express riders. Seldom staying long in one place, he rode nearly every route east of the Rockies at one time or another. For this first trip he had been chosen to make the 100-mile ride to Scott's Bluff on the North Platte River — where the Rockies reach their farthest out into the prairies.

Barely waiting for Yank to dismount, Jack flung the *mochila* over his saddle, hopped to get

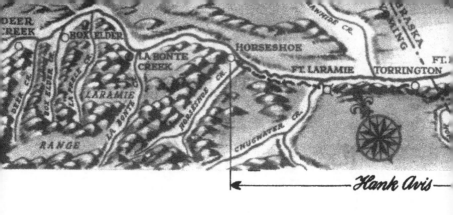

a foot in the stirrup, and was away in a shower of splashing mud. His horse, a high-spirited Thoroughbred, was nervous and eager to run, but Jack pulled him to a jolting trot. "Easy, boy. Easy," he told it. "Settle down and listen to what your Uncle Jack's a-tellin' you."

Keeping up a chatter of talk, Jack held his horse to a steady trot up the valley of Lodgepole Creek. At the first wolf howl, the horse reared and whirled to race away, but there was no break in the flow of Jack's chatter. He left the reins loose, giving his startled mount nothing to fight against. "Now look-a-here, boy," he chuckled, "that there's just a old he-wolf a-howlin' 'cause he's wet and lonesome. He don't care nothin' 'bout you and me." Within a dozen strides the

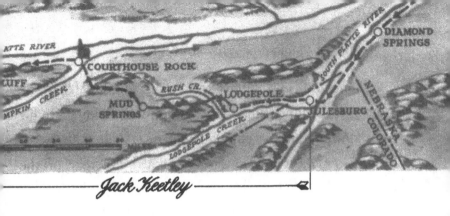

horse's fear had passed. Taking confidence from
Jack's calmness, it let itself be turned easily, then
trotted on in the blackness. At the next howl, the
Thoroughbred hardly broke the rhythm of its gait.

Leaving Lodgepole Valley on his second mount,
Jack turned well to the north, quartering into the
storm. Nervous and frightened at first, the Thoroughbred soon settled down under Jack's soothing
chatter, and held straight on at a good steady
trot. After about an hour a low roaring came
from the blackness ahead. As the sound grew
louder, Jack slowed to a jog and listened carefully.
This would be Rush Creek, usually no more than
a brook running between high banks, but now
living up to its name.

Suddenly the horse threw its head high,

snorted, and set its feet. Jack slipped from the saddle and stood for a minute, talking to his mount and stroking its muzzle. Then he led it slowly forward, angling toward the roar of the water. When the sound seemed almost under them, the horse again snorted and set its feet. Jack didn't try to hurry it on. To find a low place in the bank, and do it in the blackness, he must make full use of his horse's sight. And that sight would be worthless if the animal were excited and afraid. When the horse had calmed down, Jack led it on, walking close beside its head and crowding it gently toward the roar.

Sometimes allowing itself to be crowded, and sometimes crowding back, the horse let Jack lead it along the bank for several minutes. Then it set its feet again. This was what Jack had been waiting for. Here the creek must be overflowing a low bank. Letting the reins slip through his hand, he stepped forward cautiously into shallow water. Feeling for each step, he waded on until he reached the rein ends and felt the water up to his knees. Seeing that Jack was unharmed, the horse followed willingly into the water. Keeping up a steady chatter, Jack mounted, clucked, and turned the wading Thoroughbred gently to the right. When it stepped a foot off over the flooded bank, he cut the rein ends down sharply across its rump.

Startled, the horse lunged forward, plunged completely under the swirling water, and came up swimming desperately. It was only a moment until it was pawing wildly to climb the far bank. Diving over its head, Jack landed in knee-deep water. He scrambled quickly to his feet, and set every ounce of his hundred pounds against the bridle reins. The pull was enough to bring the struggling horse up over the steep bank.

"Easy, boy. Easy," Jack soothed the trembling Thoroughbred. "For a couple of seconds there, I didn't know if you and me was a-goin' to cross Rush Creek or the River Jordan."

Stopping only to lift the sides of the *mochila* and drain the mail cantinas of water, Jack mounted and put his horse into a smart trot. He followed Rush Creek westward for about an hour, then turned straight into the driving rain for the long climb to the top of Thirty-Mile Ridge. The

blackness was thinning to dull gray when he spied
a faint glimmer of light, ahead and off to his left.
It was just coming daylight when he rode into
Mud Springs and changed mounts. With a few

words of banter to the relay man, he cantered
away to the northwest.

At daybreak the rain slackened, but the wind
rose to a freezing gale. Here on the high divide
it cut through Jack's wet buckskins, plastering
them like a coating of ice against his body. To
protect himself as much as he could, he crouched
low on his horse's neck, using its head as a wind-
break. Now and again he slipped from the saddle,
held to a stirrup and ran to warm himself. It
seemed hours before he sighted Courthouse Rock,
standing like a great cathedral on the far side of
Pumpkin Creek.

Pumpkin Creek was running bank-full, but Jack
wasted little time in crossing it. Hitting it at an
old Indian ford, he led his nervous horse into the
shallow water, then mounted and spurred it out
into the flood. Cold as he knew the water must
be, it felt warm to him when his mount plunged
under, rose, and struck out for the far bank.

With the crossing of Pumpkin Creek, the worst
of Jack's ride was over. The last 30 miles of his
route lay on the Oregon Trail, beside the North
Platte River. There in the valley the wind was

less gusty and cold, but deep mud held his speed to a jogging trot. At 1:15 on the afternoon of April 6 he rode into Scott's Bluff and passed the *mochila* on to Hank Avis. The westbound *mochila* was now nine hours late, and Jack had lost two of those hours, but it was doubtful that many other men could have made his ride without losing at least ten.

Hank, though boyish in size and appearance, was in his middle thirties. He had been a scout with Captain Dripps's fur-trading company, and knew the country and the Indians thoroughly. His 100-mile route to Horseshoe lay through the Sioux hunting grounds, and his first relay station was at abandoned old Fort Mitchell, halfway to the Wyoming boundary. Although the mud was deep, he drove his mount hard, planning to use all its strength by the time he reached the station.

Hank was within a few miles of the old fort when he suddenly pulled his horse to a stop and jumped from the saddle. Bending low, he examined a scattering of rain-filled hoofprints that pock-marked the Oregon Trail. He read them as we read a printed page: nine Sioux Indians had raided the relay station at dawn, stolen five horses and driven them into the Wildcat Mountains. Worse still, the Indians' trail had not been followed.

Swinging back into the saddle, Hank spurred his tiring mount to a pounding gallop. At the old fort he found the stable empty. A wounded hostler and the keeper were barricaded in the station. They did not believe the Sioux tribe had gone on the warpath, but thought this to be a part of a large raiding band, out to steal a summer's supply of horses. If it was, no relay station or rider on the Oregon Trail would be safe. As there was no fresh relay and Hank's horse was already tired, they wanted him to turn back to Scott's Bluff.

Hank Avis was no man to turn back. And besides, he didn't believe the race with the Californian and Mormon riders was yet lost. There were plenty of Indians to make trouble west of the Rockies and, from the direction of the wind, the big storm might have come all the way from the Pacific Ocean. If it had, those Far Western riders might be as much as a day behind schedule.

"No," he told the keeper, "I ain't runnin' from no Injuns! With a played-out horse, I maybe can't fight 'em, but I'll bet you my spurs I can keep my hair and get past 'em."

Leaving the raided station, Hank raced his horse straight across the valley to the nearest spur of the Wildcat Mountains. After hiding it in a gulch where it could rest safely, he climbed to the top of a ridge, scanning the country to the west. When he was sure there were no Indians hidden in the valley beyond, he brought his horse up, looked carefully again, then mounted and raced for the next safe cover. By the Oregon Trail, the distance to Torrington, Wyoming, his next relay post, was 23 miles. If he stuck to the cover of the mountains he would have to ride nearly 40 miles, but that was the only safe way to go with a played-out mount.

All afternoon Hank skirted the edge of the Platte Valley, hiding his horse and scouting ahead, hill by hill. Twice he saw bands of Indians on the Oregon Trail and had to circle far back into the mountains. By the time he came out of the rough country and made his run across the valley to

Torrington Station it was two hours after dark.

The Torrington relay post was also a way station for freighters on the Oregon Trail, and was surrounded by a strong stockade. Hank found two freighting outfits forted up in the stockade, and the drivers badly frightened. They reported bands of mounted Sioux all along the trail to the west, some of them in war paint.

Hank wouldn't even stop for coffee. The storm seemed to be breaking a little and he was anxious to be on his way. He knew these outlying foothills of the Rockies as well as a villager knows his home town. With a few stars to guide himself by, he could easily get around any Indians camped along the trail.

The horse Hank drew at Torrington was strong and willing, and he pushed it along at as fast a pace as the rough going would allow. Back in the hills he had little worry of running into an ambush, and made the 30-mile ride to Fort Laramie in less than four hours. It was just midnight when he blew his horn to wake Seth Ward, the stationkeeper.

"What in tarnation be you a-doin' here?" Seth

shouted as he opened the gate. "Don't you know there's Injun raiders scattered all abouts?"

"Ain't saw an Injun since ever I crossed the Newbrasky line," Hank shouted back. "Rassle me out a horse — and a good one! The way I'm a-goin' it'll be thirty tough miles to Horseshoe."

From Fort Laramie to Horseshoe Station, there was little place for a rider to keep hidden. The country was open rolling prairie, and even in starlight a rider could be seen at a long distance. Again Hank went back to leaving his horse and scouting from each hilltop before he crossed it. Two or three times he spied a flicker of light from an Indian campfire, and had to ride far around it, but he wasted no minute that he could help. At 4:30 on the morning of April 7 he rode his well-spent horse into the Horseshoe relay station. The westbound mail was now 12 hours late, but the race was far from over.

Mormon Riders of the Desert

10

It almost seemed that the weather, as well as the Indians, had conspired against the first riders of the Pony Express. Spring showers are to be expected along the valley of the Platte River, but storms lasting several days are uncommon. In the deserts they are almost unheard of. Springtime there is usually bright and sunny, often hot. But in April of 1860 storm clouds stretched across the whole western half of the continent, bringing with them pitch-black nights, blizzards, and endless days of heavy rain.

From the time the eastbound mail had left San Francisco, the only break in the clouds had been at Lake Tahoe. When, at 9 o'clock on the morning of April 6, Jay Kelley passed the *mochila* on to "Wash" Perkins at Ruby Valley, a cold rain was setting in.

Ruby Valley was the dividing point between the California and Mormon riders, and the rivalry between them was keen. They would stand together in the race against the riders to the east of the Rockies, but each group was determined to set the fastest record on its section of the trail. To Wash Perkins, still in his teens, it seemed that the rain had held off just long enough to ruin the Mormon boys' chance against the Californians.

Major Howard Egan was superintendent of the Mormon division of the Pony Express. He had pioneered most of the Pony trail across the deserts and badlands, built the relay stations, and carefully chosen the riders from among the members of his own church. Each one was a boy in his late teens, light in weight, fearless, trail-wise, honest, and determined to prove that the Mormon horsemen were the best in the world. To help his riders, Major Egan had supplied them with the finest horses in the Mormon stables, and divided the 242-mile trail between Ruby Valley and Camp

Floyd into four short routes.

The trail laid out for Wash Perkins' route to Schell Creek was little more than 60 miles long, but crossed two alkali flats and three rugged mountain chains. When practicing, Wash had twice ridden the route in five hours. As he snatched the *mochila* from Jay and raced away from the Ruby Valley station, he made up his mind to beat that record in spite of the rain.

Bent low in his saddle, Wash streaked across Ruby Valley, heading straight for the canyon that led steeply up to the pass across the first mountain range. But with every stride of his pony the rain fell harder. It had become a deluge by the time he raced into the canyon mouth, and a shallow creek was rushing down the trail. Wash paid no attention to the water, but whipped his pony through it and splashed on toward the steep rise to the pass. He fought his way upward until he was halfway to the summit. There the canyon narrowed and the creek became a raging torrent, too swift for the pony to climb through. After his mount had fallen twice, Wash had no choice but to turn back to the valley.

With nearly an hour lost in trying to get over the mountains, Wash was disappointed but not discouraged. Although he would miss both of his relay posts and have no change of mounts, he would add only 20 miles to his ride by circling the ends of the ranges. The scheduled time for his route was nine hours, and he believed he could still reach Schell Creek on time. He might have made it if after the first downpour the storm hadn't settled into a steady, soaking rain that turned the alkali flats into hoof-deep mud. Even though he had no Indian trouble, and the ride he made that day was a marvelous one, it was deep twilight before he reached Schell Creek.

Darkness and steady rain were falling when Jim Gentry took the *mochila* from Wash. Jim's 60-mile trail lay through the desolate Antelope Mountains, across 24 miles of badlands, over another high ridge, and down to Deep Creek relay station in Utah Territory. By looking at the Pony Express schedule, anyone unfamiliar with the route might have believed that nine hours had been allowed for the eastbound run, but this was not the case. The time zone follows the Utah-Nevada line, so Jim would lose an hour through starting his ride by Pacific Time and ending it by Mountain Time, which is an hour later.

Under good conditions, this loss of an hour would not have bothered Jim. Although the country was rugged, his trail was a reasonably easy one in daylight and fair weather — he had made several practice runs in five hours each — but in dead blackness and rain the ride could be

almost a nightmare. He was anxious and watchful as he rode away into the storm.

Regardless of the weather, Indians lay in wait for Jim at the pass through the Antelopes. He saw none of them, but the flicker of their camp-fires drove him far from the trail, into wilderness where every step was treacherous. Six or seven times his pony slipped and went down in the grease-slick mud of the badlands. Each time the pony got up unhurt, and Jim was able to jump clear, but he was definitely worried. A horse could easily break a leg in those quick falls, and without the help of its sight in that blackness, the chance of getting the mail through would be small. There would be no possibility of reaching

Let Harrington ──→ Billy Fisher

a relay station before morning, and, afoot in daylight, there would be no hope of escaping the Indians.

It was 6:10 A.M. by the keeper's watch when Jim rode into the Deep Creek station, dead tired and covered from head to heels with mud. His knowledge of the badlands, good luck, and the sturdiness of his ponies were all that had saved the mail, but more than three hours had been lost on the scheduled time for his run.

Taking the mud-smeared *mochila* from Jim Gentry, "Let" Huntington carried it over a 6000-foot pass in the Deep Creek Mountains and down to the Great Salt Lake Desert. In dry weather he could have raced straight across to his home station at. Simpson's Spring. But the rain had turned the desert into a sea of salt-crusted putty-like mud that would cripple a horse within a mile or two. Let had no choice but to circle the salt flats, hugging close to the base of the surrounding mountains — and each one of them proved to be an Indian ambush.

Let Huntington's reputation as a crack shot was well known to the Indians. They had no courage to meet him in the open, but from ambush they used him for target practice. Hemmed in by mountains on one side and salt flats on the other, he could not avoid the ambushes. His only defense was to fling himself along the far side of his pony, race past each one, and outdistance any mounted Indians that followed him.

This was one time when the Indians helped to speed the Pony Express: they kept Let racing for his life. With two changes of mounts he ran every gantlet safely and, at noon, turned the *mochila* over to Billy Fisher at Simpson's Spring.

Billy Fisher was to see plenty of Indian trouble in the months ahead, but he had none on his ride to Camp Floyd, the Army post near the western shore of Utah Lake. Instead he had rain, mud, and disappointment. His route lay through the rich farmlands of Rush Valley, softened into black muck. One of the fastest of the Mormon riders, he had determined to set a record on this run, but the ride he hoped to make in four hours took seven. It was 6:30 on the night of April 7 when he brought his plodding pony into Camp Floyd. To Billy, the race with the riders from the East seemed hopelessly lost.

11

J IM G ENTRY was still floundering through the grease-slick badlands of Nevada when, at 4:30 on the morning of April 7, Hank Avis galloped his spent pony into Horseshoe Station, high in the Wyoming foothills of the Rockies.

"Watch out for Sioux, they're thicker'n fleas on a coyote!" Hank shouted to Bill Cates as he sprang from the saddle. "You fight shy o' the trail, and keep a sharp eye peeled, kid!"

Bill slapped the *mochila* across his saddle and vaulted up, but before opening the gate to let him out, the old keeper shouted, "Don't you pay him no mind, Billy! Just like I been tellin' you, there's a blizzard a-comin' on, but it'll be mostly this side o' Deer Creek. Injuns knows enough to hole up in a blizzard; you stick to the trail an' burn leather for Platte Bridge!"

Bill Cates, just out of his teens, was an Illinois plainsman, but he had been in the Rockies two years and knew the Oregon Trail well. What he didn't know was whether to follow the advice of the weather-wise old keeper or the cautioning of Hank Avis, one of the best scouts in the Rockies. The blackness of the night convinced him to take the keeper's advice — at least, on the 20-mile ride to La Bonte Creek, his first relay post. He held close to the Oregon Trail, saw no Indian campfires, and drove his mount to the very limit of its strength. Daylight came when he was halfway, and with it a freezing wind sprang up, whipping icy particles of snow before it.

At La Bonte Creek the Platte River turns sharply to the north, circling the Laramie, Haystack, and Casper mountain ranges. To follow the river around would make Bill's ride to Box Elder Station 30 miles. By striking due west and hugging the foothills, he could cut the distance to 20, and believed he could outrun the blizzard that was surely coming. Beyond Box Elder, he'd have only a 10-mile ride to Deer Creek, then 30 more to Platte Bridge.

Bill laid the rein ends sharply across his mount's rump, lifting the pony into a sharp gallop and heading straight for the foothills. He'd not only outrun the storm; he'd make Platte Bridge by noon and be in Red Buttes, his home station, by 1:30. Let's see . . . that would knock three hours off the scheduled time for his run. This race with the Californians and Mormons wasn't lost yet — not by a little brown jugful!

Bill was so busy with his thinking that he didn't notice the increasing violence of the storm until he had reached the base of the Laramies. To protect himself and his horse, he reined closer in among the foothills. Within a half-hour the wind was so filled with snow that he could see no more than twenty rods, and in the rough going his horse began to tire rapidly. He had to let it slow down to a trot, then to a jog.

Within another hour Bill began to worry. The wind seemed to have gone crazy. It was veering wildly, striking from either side and straight on, and it was impossible to tell direction by it. Any way he turned, he found a rocky hillside, snow was piling up in the gulches, and he could barely see sixty feet. He had turned his tired horse and was trying to find his way out of the foothills when he discovered a rapidly flowing creek. "Doggone!" he shouted. "Don't reckon I was so far off at that! This here'll be Box Elder Creek. All I got to do is foller it down to the depot."

Hour after hour Bill followed the creek out of the foothills and across a wide valley. Shivering, he pulled the buckskins high around his neck, hunched his head, and kept his weary horse going at the best pace it could manage in the deepening snow. He had lost all track of time, and his mind was numb with cold when he came to the end of the creek. It emptied into the Platte, just above a downstream bend to the right.

Bill Cates needed no one to tell him that he had never reached the Box Elder, but had followed La Prele Creek to the northeast and was little nearer Red Buttes than he had been at dawn. In his drowsiness he had crossed the snow-

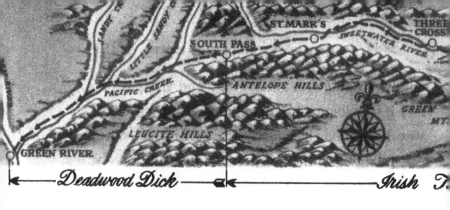

covered Oregon Trail without seeing it, and had ridden nearly ten miles beyond.

Twilight was falling when Bill at last reached Box Elder Station. He was already two hours overdue at Red Buttes, but more than 50 miles of blizzard-ridden trail still lay ahead of him. Half frozen and starved, he would neither stop to get warm nor let the keeper carry the mail on for him. Gulping down a few mouthfuls of antelope stew, he swung onto his saddle and rode back into the storm.

Although the wind was still strong and snow-filled, there were no deep drifts in the Platte River valley. Leaving Box Elder, Bill stuck close to the Oregon Trail and kept his horse at a steady trot. Night overtook him long before he reached Deer Creek, but with darkness the wind eased.

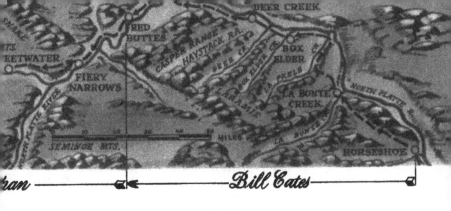

Beyond Deer Creek the air cleared, the blackness of the night faded, and here and there a star peeped through the clouds. With each mile that Bill rode, the depth of snow on the ground lessened; the blizzard hadn't reached this far to the northwest.

"Durned bighead!" Bill mumbled to himself. "If I'd a-listened to the old man and not tried to cut corners, I'd have outrode that blizzard and been in Red Buttes hours ago. Well, what's done is done, and there's no use bawlin' over it. Git along, old pony! There's hay in the barn at Platte Bridge."

When an hour before midnight he rode into Platte Bridge Station, the whole sky was a-twinkle with stars. Across the river and up on a fine horse, he set out rapidly on the last leg of his route. In the bright starlight he had no trouble in following the Oregon Trail, and his mount held willingly to a good pace. But by the time he reached Red Buttes and tossed the *mochila* to "Irish Tommy" Ranahan, the mail was nearly 20 hours behind schedule.

Irish Tommy — little, bowlegged, and spry as a grasshopper — was no boy. Ever since the California gold discovery he had been guide, bull whacker, mule skinner, or stage driver on the Oregon Trail. He knew the Sweetwater River valley as no other man knew it, and called it his stomping ground. If the whole world had been searched, no better man could have been found to carry the Pony Mail to the top of the Continental Divide. His 140-mile route to South Pass was the longest, and one of the most dangerous, in the entire 1966 miles of the Pony Express trail. He had no use for race horses, but demanded mustangs as rough as the country they would be running through.

When, from half a mile away, Tommy heard the sound of Bill Cates's horn, he ran for the corral with his rope swinging. By the time Bill rode in, a mustang was saddled, bridled, and a helper was holding it by the ears so it couldn't fight. Bill's boots had barely touched the ground before Tommy grabbed the *mochila*, flung it over his saddle, and vaulted up. With his feet still feeling for the stirrups, he shouted, "Turn him loose and let him shake!"

The helper let go and jumped back, the station-keeper swung the corral gate open, and the wildly bucking bronco went through it like a cat in a fit. Flailing his hat and shrieking like an Indian on the warpath, Irish Tommy spurred the mustang from shoulder to rump. Unable to shake him loose, the bronco tried to run away from the biting spurs. Crowhopping through the stockade gate, it raced up the trail at breakneck speed.

Tommy stopped spurring as soon as the bronco settled into a run, but he didn't try to slow it down or spare it. This was a Wyoming badlands mustang, used to taking care of itself. He'd run until a man might think he was ready to drop, but he'd always keep back a reserve of hidden strength.

From Red Buttes the trail twisted upward

along the edge of the rushing Platte River, hugging close to the foot of the Rattlesnake mountain range. With four or five inches of snow on the ground, it was a climb that would have tired most horses within a few miles — but not this badlands mustang. As soon as he was away from the station he settled into a steady lope, breaking it only at the steepest climbs or to flounder through snowdrifts. Tommy expected no Indian trouble, but from habit his eyes searched the mountainside ahead. Unlike Jack Keetley, Tommy rode in silence, and with snow to muffle his pony's hoofbeats, they moved soundlessly through the starry night.

At the Fiery Narrows, 30 miles out of Red Buttes, the mustang dropped its head and began to weave in its gait. Knowing that it still had a reserve of strength, Tommy spurred the bronco sharply, running it hard for the last two miles into Sweetwater relay station.

With a stout mustang under him, Tommy left the Platte and turned into the foothills of the Granite Mountains, following up the north bank of Sweetwater River. Here the trail was rough and dangerous, but the run to Devil's Gate was only 20 miles, and Tommy kept his pony at a brisk canter. Nearly two hours later, and in the dim gray light of early morning, he passed Independence Rock — the great landmark of the Oregon Trail where hundreds of emigrants had stopped to scratch their names in the granite. Daylight had broken clear and cold when he circled Devil's Gate and cantered his exhausted pony into his second relay station.

Irish Tommy's third mustang was even wilder than his first. It had taken four men to saddle it, and it left the Devil's Gate station in an explosion of frantic bucking, but Tommy would have no other horse. Ahead lay the 28 most rugged miles of his route, and it would take a tough bronco to run it at a speed of nine miles an hour. The trail clung tight against the rocky rim of the Granite range, the climbs were steep, and at Three Crossings the river snaked through a canyon so narrow that three fordings had to be made within a mile. Tommy allowed himself three hours for the ride, and reached the Three Crossings station almost on the minute.

From Three Crossings westward, the Sweet-water River valley spread out into broad meadows where great herds of deer, elk, and antelope grazed. This was easy going. There was little snow on the trail, and Tommy held his mount to a steady canter, covering the 32 miles to the St. Mark's relay post in 3½ hours.

Irish Tommy had already put 110 miles behind him, enough to wear out any man, and 30 more still lay ahead. Stopping at St. Mark's only long enough to wolf down a bowl of venison stew, he swung back into the saddle and hit the trail for South Pass — the top of the Continental Divide and the end of his route.

At St. Mark's the green meadows were left behind, and dry, rolling prairies rose in steps to the top of the Divide. Off to the south the Antelope Hills raised their snowy tops against the clear sky. And from the north a cutting wind swept down from the high Wind River Mountains.

For this last climb, Tommy had chosen a strong, well-knit mustang, and planned to spare it a little on the early part of his ride. He was sitting loose in the saddle, half drowsing, when suddenly he came to attention. He shaded his eyes and carefully examined a dry gulch ahead and off to his left. He could see nothing, but was sure his eye had caught some movement there. Caution, born of long years in the mountains, warned him. He touched spurs to his pony and turned it off the trail, giving the gulch a wide berth.

Suddenly, as if boiling out of the ground, a band of yelling Indians raced their ponies out of the gulch. "Shoshones!" Tommy muttered to himself, dropped low in the saddle and spurred sharply. Gathering its muscles, his mustang leaped away in a burst of speed. Then, from behind, the sound of rifle fire cut through the yelling. Tommy was no more afraid than if the Indians had been shooting popguns at him. He glanced back over his shoulder just long enough to be sure his mustang was outdistancing the Indian ponies.

As the Indians gave up the chase, Tommy shouted a few choice insults at them, then swung his pony back to the trail and rode on as though nothing had happened. At 4:50 on the afternoon

of April 8, he slid his sweat-streaked mustang to a stop in front of the South Pass relay station. He had ridden his whole route in exactly the scheduled time — but the westbound mail was still nearly 20 hours late.

"Shake a leg now, lad!" Tommy shouted to "Deadwood Dick" as he hauled the *mochila* off his saddle. "This race ain't over yet! Not at all, at all! Like as not them Mormon boys is bogged down in the mud o' Great Salt Lake. It's all downhill from here to Bear River, bub, and we got 'em licked!"

The Mormon Riders of Utah

12

WHEN, AT 6:30 on the rain-swept night of April 7, Billy Fisher plodded into Camp Floyd, Major Howard Egan flung the eastbound *mochila* across his own saddle, mounted, and galloped away into the darkness. Since there was no faster means of communication than the Pony Riders themselves, he had no way of knowing that the storm extended halfway across the continent, that the riders east of the Rockies had been running late, or that Bill Cates had spent most of the day lost in a blizzard.

For all Major Egan knew, a westbound rider might already be across South Pass and racing toward the goal at the Bear River ford. Actually, the Western riders were well ahead of schedule. Bart Riles and Jay Kelley had lost little more than half of the time gained in the amazing ride that the California boys had made to Fort Churchill. Then too, Let Huntington had made up all the time lost by Jim Gentry. But the Major was greatly concerned by his Mormon riders' having fallen far behind his expectations. Some desperate riding would have to be done if the Mormons were to hold up their end of the race — riding more dangerous than he would assign to any man but himself.

A fine paved highway now connects Utah Lake and Salt Lake City. In 1860 a rough Army road followed the same route, and the creeks and rivers were bridged. With reins barely taut enough to help a stumbling horse catch its balance, the Major turned onto the Army road. Salt Lake City lay 75 miles to the north, and two fast horses were waiting at relay stations, evenly spaced along the way.

Unable to see his own hands in the blackness, Major Egan kept his mount at the fastest pace its strength could endure for a 25-mile run. Although he knew that one misstep in the sloppy going might break both their necks, he gave his horse free rein, trusting thoroughly in its sight and intelligence.

Good horses are like good men. They know instinctively when genuine confidence is placed in them, and repay it with their finest efforts. All three horses Major Egan rode that night were top-string, and they repaid his trust with every ounce of their strength and courage.

The Major had saved his fastest and toughest mount for the home stretch. It was a high-strung, wiry plains pony, and held to a pounding gallop for the first 23 miles of its relay. Then, two miles away, the lights of Salt Lake City suddenly showed through the blackness. A moment later Major Egan heard his pony's hoofs clatter on the plank bridge over Mill Creek. Instantly, the saddle dropped from under him, water splashed into his face and swirled around his knees, but he kept his seat.

The bridge was at a curve in the road, just beyond a willow thicket. The speeding pony, glancing up when the lights came into view, had

overshot the bridge and leaped off into the creek. Without losing its footing, it scrambled up the bank, caught its stride, and galloped on to the home station at the Salt Lake House.

The chime clock in the lobby was just striking 11:45 when Major Howard Egan pulled up at the hotel entrance. One of the greatest horsemen of all time, he had ridden 75 miles through mud, rain, and darkness in 5 hours and 15 minutes — cutting the scheduled time for his route by more than half. The ride he made that storm-lashed night will long stand as a landmark in American horsemanship and courage.

"Ras" Egan took the *mochila* from his father at the Salt Lake House, but he had no military road to follow eastward through the high Wasatch Mountains. His route was along the deep wheel ruts of the old Mormon Trail. Climbing high on a mountainside, he left the lights of the city behind and plunged into the blackness of Emigration Canyon. Barely wide enough in some places to let a wagon through, the canyon wound between towering rock walls to Donner Hill at its far end. A trot was the best pace Ras could hold through the gorge, up Donner Hill, and over Little Mountain.

In the darkness and rain, the stiff climb to the crest of Big Mountain had to be made step by slow step. Trying to make up time, Ras put his pony down the far side at a dangerous trot, then turned onto Dutchman's Flat. Rich black farmland, the flat was soaked until it had become a bog of foot-deep gummy mud. There was no way around, and the pony could wade no more than forty lengths without a rest. The sky was turning gray in the east when Ras brought his exhausted mount into the relay station at Snyder's Mill. In 5 hours of hard riding he had covered barely 25 miles.

With a fast pony under him, Dutchman's Flat behind, and daylight coming on, Ras Egan set out to make up some of the time he had lost. The rain was letting up a little and, with a relay at Dixie Creek, there was no need to spare his ponies. Bent low in his saddle, and coaxing every possible inch of speed from his mounts, Ras streaked across the hills, through the cheering little settlement of Webster, past Hanging Rock, and between the high red cliffs of Echo Canyon.

There was no hope of equaling his father's record, but together the Egans had nearly halved the good-weather schedule on their runs. In 12½ hours they had carried the mail 125 miles over one of the country's highest mountain chains, through darkness, mud, and pouring rain. It was a few minutes before seven when Ras reined in his dripping pony at the Echo Canyon relay station and tossed the *mochila* to Tom King.

Tom was in his late teens, weighed barely a hundred pounds, and was noted for being the fastest rider among all the Mormon boys. It was for this reason that Major Egan had chosen him for this particular route. His was the sprint run. Midway to Fort Bridger his trail crossed Bear River — goal in the race against the riders from east of the Rockies.

The first 30 miles of Tom's route lay through rough country on the eastern slope of the mountains, but he kept his pony at a stiff gallop over most of the way. At any time now the rider from the east might be expected to reach Bear River

and, with the race so nearly won, Tom had no intention of being beaten. With a change of mounts at Needle Rock, he climbed to the high Wasatch Pass at a horse-killing trot. From the summit he could see far over into Wyoming Territory. Between, flowed Bear River, but the trail on either side was hidden by hills or woods. Tom knew that somewhere along that unseen strip of trail a rider might be driving desperately for the goal, and that the race could yet be lost.

He urged his leg-weary pony down from the pass at a speed that was close to being foolhardy. After reaching the valley he kept the line ends slashing. The ford was only a half mile ahead, but cottonwoods along the river still hid it from sight. He could not be sure that the Western

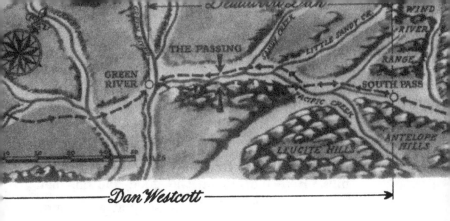

riders had won the race until his pony galloped between the trees and the rain-swollen river lay before him. Then, horseman that he was, he cooled the sweating pony out before putting it through the ice-cold water.

Even though the race with the Eastern riders had been won, the big race — the race against time — was still far from finished. Unless the mail was delivered at each end of the 1966-mile trail within the ten-day limit set by Mr. Russell, his promise to the United States Government would be broken, and the Pony Express might become a failure. But the riders of the Pony Express would sacrifice their lives before they would accept failure. Regardless of weather, danger, or what route must be ridden, there would be no letting up until the whole job was done — and done well.

When Tom King rode out of Bear River valley, Wyoming lay before him in great gully-slashed hills. Here the footing was good, the rain had stopped, and Tom kept his pony at a swinging canter. The sun was less than an hour past mid-sky when he forded Muddy Creek, made a quick relay, and galloped away on the last leg of his route to Jim Bridger's old fort.

Dan Westcott was waiting anxiously when Tom rode in. For hours he'd been watching the trail, but there was still no sign of the overdue rider with the mail from St. Joseph. "Bet a hat I beat him to Green River," he shouted as he swung into the saddle and galloped away down Black Fork Creek.

Dan's pony was a tough, hard-bitted badlands mustang, but he held it down to a swinging canter. The run to Granger Settlement, his first relay post, was 30 miles, and there was nothing between but coyotes, antelope, and prairie. Ten miles an hour was as fast as he dared let the mustang go. A played-out pony in that lonely country could delay the mail for hours — and cost him a long, long walk.

Everyone in Granger was gathered around the relay station when Dan cantered in, swung the *mochila* over the saddle of his relief pony, and galloped away. Now, with a fresh horse waiting at Rock Ridge, and another at the Green River crossing, he could turn on the speed. The sun was already low in the west, and he wanted to gain every mile he could before darkness fell. Leaving Black Fork valley, he spurred up the long divide to Rock Ridge, made a lightning-fast relay and raced down to the valley of the Green.

Tossing the *mochila* upon a waiting mount, Dan crossed Green River and turned up the Big Sandy toward South Pass. The trail followed the river valley all the way to Big Sandy stage station, but Dan didn't. By cutting straight across the hills and making two or three extra fordings he could save several miles. He had made his first cutoff, forded the river, and was well up the next hill when, from the valley below, he heard the music of a running horse's hoofs. "Yaa-hooo, Pony!" he hooted into the darkness.

A moment later Deadwood Dick's answer came back, almost like an echo, "Yaa-hooo, Pony!" Unseen, the riders from East and West had passed where only the coyotes could hear their hooted greeting.

In the months that were to come, the riders from east of the Rockies would win many a race, but all the glory of the first one belonged to the Californians and Mormons. The eastbound mail was more than 14 hours ahead of schedule when the riders passed, shortly after nine o'clock on the night of April 8, and the westbound mail was nearly 20 hours late. The deep mud and wild country had proved to be too much for the fine-bred Eastern race horses, while the tough Western mustangs had more than met every demand made upon them. But the race between the riders and horses of East and West was of little moment. The big race against time had yet to be won.

The big race was won — gloriously. And again all the honors went to the Westerners. Racing the St. Joseph mail westward across mountains and deserts, they made up time on every relay until, at last, the whole 20 hours had been whittled away. At 5:30 P.M. on April 13 — 9 days, 15 hours, and 15 minutes from the time he had dashed away with the eastbound *mochila* — Sam Hamilton galloped back into Sacramento with the first Pony Express Mail from the East. This time a cheering throng jammed J Street, and a wildly shouting troop of horsemen hemmed Sam in from either side.

While the Mormons and Californians had been racing toward Sacramento, the prairie riders were fighting their way eastward through still-deep mud. Although they lost most of the time originally gained by the Westerners, they brought the San Francisco mail into St. Joseph well ahead of schedule. At 3:55 P.M. on April 13, Johnny Frey — again rigged out in his fancy clothes — clattered up Jule Street, leaped from the saddle, and passed the *mochila* into Mr. Russell's waiting hands.

The riders of the Pony Express — both east and west of the Rockies — had proved that, in spite of rain, mud, blizzards, and Indians, the mail could go through in the ten days William Russell had promised.

THE PONY EXPRESS was established at the most dangerous period in Nevada history. From the time the first explorers made their way across the Great Basin, the Paiute Indians had been unfriendly. Often abused by gold seekers on their way to California, their hatred for white men had grown steadily. Then, in 1859, rich gold and silver deposits were discovered in their homeland. Carson City and Virginia City sprang up and hundreds of prospectors poured in, swarming through the hills, killing the game, and cutting down the nut trees that furnished most of the Paiutes' food.

About the time the first Pony Express mail was

carried, Chief Winnemucca called a great war council at Pyramid Lake, and the Indians determined to drive every white man from their homeland. Forty-six miners were killed in an ambush, and when word of the disaster reached California, a detachment of U.S. troops was sent to punish the Paiutes. The soldiers, unfamiliar with the country, were never able to catch the Indians, and only succeeded in scattering them into hiding on the deserts. There they took out their spite by destroying lonely Pony Express relay stations and harrassing the riders. Station after station was sent up in smoke, the keepers were killed and the relay horses stolen.

By the middle of May in 1860 the Paiute campaign against the Pony Express was at its fiercest. Most of the Nevada relay stations had been destroyed and ambushes set in nearly every mountain pass, canyon and thicket along the whole length of the route. Trying to carry mail over it was like running a 500-mile gantlet. The work of the Pony Express riders became almost a nightmare, but there is only one record of a rider refusing to make his run or turning back because he was afraid.

Often when a rider finished his route on a tired horse, he found his home station destroyed and had to ride on for another 25 or 50 miles. The riders avoided the regular trail as much as possible, seldom following the same route twice, and made their runs far out among the desert hills. But, to change horses, they were forced to come in to the few remaining relay stations. And there were several ambush spots that could not be avoided. Quaking Aspen Bottom was the most dangerous of all. It was a Paiute stronghold, and there was no way around it.

With two mails each way to be carried every week, the strain on the Nevada riders was terrific. Although only one rider was killed while on the trail, several were badly wounded, and others became so worn out that they were unable to climb into a saddle. Those who were still fit often rode double routes, to keep the mail going through as nearly on schedule as possible.

In early May, Jay Kelley made one of the longest, fastest, and most dangerous double runs. At dawn he finished his regular 116-mile ride from Ruby Valley, and rolled into his bunk at Smith's Creek. At two o'clock that afternoon another *mochila* was brought in from the east. There was no other rider to take it over the 117-mile "Ambush Trail" to Fort Churchill, so Jay saddled and was away within two minutes. He spared his pony until he reached Quaking Aspen Bottom, then shot through the ambush at a dead run.

Crossing the Desatoya Mountains high above the regular pass, he sneaked into Cold Spring for a change of ponies, then raced on. A few miles to the west he rounded a mountain shoulder and came suddenly upon a wagon train of frightened emigrants who were trying to get out of the country. They opened fire the moment Jay rode into sight — and they were excellent shots. Bullets screeched within inches of his head, and he had to ride for his life to get past without being killed.

Jay reached Fort Churchill at midnight, and had slept less than four hours when Bob Haslam brought in the eastbound mail from Friday's Station. At the sound of Bob's war whoop, Jay sprang from his bunk, wide awake and pulling on his boots. Two minutes later he was in the saddle again and galloping back east toward the aspen thickets in Carson River Marsh. To get through the ambush before daylight, he took the trail at reckless speed, risking the possibility that his pony might fail to make a sharp bend and be mired in a bog.

Out of the marsh at dawn, Jay made a quick relay at Stillwater and passed Sand Springs soon after sunrise. He was halfway to Cold Spring when he again came upon the emigrants, camped with their wagons drawn into a circle and sentries posted. Still angry, Jay rode into their camp, shouting that he was an American and demanding to know why they had shot at him the day before.

"Was that you we shot at?" they asked in surprise. "The way you was ridin' we was sure you was an Injun."

Burned brown by the desert sun, and usually dressed in ragged buckskins, Jay did look like an Indian — and he rode like one. At Cold Spring he chose the fastest horse in the corral, spared it carefully in the rugged 12-mile climb over the Desatoyas, then raced it through Quaking Aspen Bottom. At such a speed, and lying against his pony's neck, he made so poor a target that no shot was fired at him. Out of the ambush thicket and safely up the trail, he stopped to let his winded pony catch its breath. As he looked back he could see the treetops being swayed by the Indians running among the slender trunks. A few days later two U.S. soldiers were killed while trying to run that ambush.

With Quaking Aspen Bottom passed, Jay let his pony climb the Shoshone range at an easy pace. He was beginning to get a bit tired himself. It was two o'clock in the afternoon when he reached Smith's Creek and crawled back into the bunk he had left just 24 hours before. But in that 24 hours he had made the longest single day's ride — 234 miles — ever made by a Pony Express rider.

When the Indian trouble was at its height, Wash Perkins and Billy Fisher doubled up on the Ruby Valley run, and barely got through alive. Every relay station for more than 100 miles had been destroyed, so they had no change of mounts. All through the night Indian fires burned along the trail, forcing them back among the desert hills. At daylight signal smokes rose all around them. Ducking, dodging, avoiding ambush spots, and often having to race for their lives, they kept out of rifle and arrow range until nearly noon.

Then, when they were within 20 miles of the end of their route, they had to cross a high mountain range. The only possible way was through a pass that they knew would be ambushed. At its narrowest point the canyon was choked by cedar thickets crowded close to the trail. Wash and Billy rode cautiously until they reached the cedars, then struck spurs to their horses. At the same moment a swarm of yelling Indians sprang from behind the trees. Rifles barked, bowstrings twanged, and bullets and arrows whizzed around the boys' heads. A bullet ripped through the top of Billy's *mochila*. An arrow pinned Wash's pants-leg to his saddle. But their horses, spent as they already were, carried them through and outran the Indian ponies.

These Pony Express horses had heart and

courage to match that of the men who rode them.
Wash Perkins had ridden one of the finest on the
line. It took him through to the end of his run
without a falter, but it never walked again. It
had given willingly every ounce of its strength

and its life. The next morning its muscles were set as solidly as stone. It couldn't be led from the stall, and died standing on its feet.

Many of the Pony Express riders escaped death by narrow margins, but Nick Wilson's was the narrowest. Nick was a Mormon boy in his late teens. Riding into Spring Valley relay station, he found no keeper waiting with a fresh horse. Since the station was not burned and a few relay horses were grazing nearby, he did not suspect an Indian attack. Jumping to the ground, he unsaddled and started to the stable for a remount. He was nearly there when he heard a war whoop, and looked up to see two Indians driving away the relay horses.

Yanking the six-shooter from his belt, Nick raced after the Indians, shouting and shooting as he ran. Well out of range, they trotted the horses toward a cedar-covered hilltop. Nick should have suspected an ambush, but he was too determined to get the horses back. He was gaining on the thieves, and without any thought of danger chased them into the cedar grove. He had barely run in among the trees when an Indian leaped into his path. Before Nick could raise his six-shooter a stone-tipped arrow was flying at his head. His last memory was of trying to dodge it.

Fortunately, two boys who were making their way out of the desert found Nick a few hours later. The arrow had struck him two inches above the left eye, and more than half of the arrowhead was buried in his skull. The boys tried to pull it out, but only managed to pull the shaft out of the stone tip. They were sure Nick was already dying, but rolled him into the shade and hurried to the next relay station for help.

Next morning when two men rode out to bury the dead Pony rider, they found Nick still breathing, though unconscious. They tied him across a saddle and took him to Ruby Valley, with no expectation of his living out the long trip. Again he surprised them. A doctor took out the arrowhead and patched him up. In a few days he regained consciousness; and in a few weeks he was back riding the Pony Express. Nick Wilson lived to be a very old man, but he always wore his hat cocked low above his left eye, to cover the deep hole made by the arrowhead.

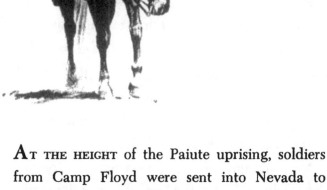

14

AT THE HEIGHT of the Paiute uprising, soldiers from Camp Floyd were sent into Nevada to punish the Indians. Being unfamiliar with the deserts, the officers often called upon Bart Riles to guide them.

At noon on May 15, 1860, Bart had just returned to Smith's Creek from an 85-mile guiding trip when a rider brought in the westbound mail. Stopping only to saddle his favorite Appaloosa pony, Bart took the *mochila* and cantered away on the 117-mile Ambush Trail to Fort Churchill.

He quit the trail soon after leaving Smith's Creek, circled far to the north, and began climbing the Shoshone mountain range cautiously. He planned to save enough of his pony's strength for a fast drive through Quaking Aspen Bottom, but the Indians had ambushed every pass in the Shoshones. Three times Bart was forced to outrace a band of well-armed warriors, and by the time he reached the thicket his pony was too leg-weary for a fast run.

Bart had barely entered the aspen thicket when an arrow whistled past his face. Ahead he could see no more than fifteen yards down the winding trail. But there, two warriors stood blocking his way with drawn bows. Dropping flat on his pony's neck, Bart charged them fiercely, hurrying their shots and making them miss. Spurring desperately, he drove his tired pony on at the very limit of its speed. From both sides of the trail arrows whizzed past them, and rifles blasted from no more than two or three yards away.

Halfway through the thicket the pony staggered, nearly fell, then regained its feet and plunged on heavily. Glancing back, Bart saw that the white patch on its rump was streaming blood. A bullet had ripped across it, laying the hide open as if cut by a knife. Bart stopped spurring and urged the pony on with his voice. It was doing its best and there was no sense in punishing it with the spurs. With every sharp twist in the trail, the pony staggered, faltered, and drove on at a slower pace.

The trees were thinning and the end of the thicket was only yards away when Bart was nearly knocked from the saddle. There was no sharp pain, but he felt as if he had been hit in the side with a sledge hammer. He grabbed for the saddle horn with both hands as a bright light flashed before his eyes. Blackness closed in around the brightness, squeezing it down until only a speck remained. Then the speck flickered out.

When Bart came to, his hands were locked to the saddle horn, and his pony was struggling up the steep trail toward the pass through the Desatoya Mountains. It was only then that Bart realized he had been shot. A burning, aching pain dragged at his stomach. From above each hip blood oozed down the legs of his buckskins and dripped onto the *mochila*.

Dimly Bart realized that a bullet, fired from close range, had passed clear through him. He knew he was dying, but tried to shake the dizziness from his head, took off his neckerchief, tore it in half, and plugged the holes in his sides. Then, slowly and fumblingly, he ripped the hem from his jacket, tied it around his waist and knotted himself tightly to the saddle horn. It was still ten miles to Cold Spring, and he knew he could never stay conscious to get there. If he fell from his pony it would stop or leave the trail and the mail would be destroyed by the Indians. If he could keep his body in the saddle, whether unconscious or dead, the pony would stick to the trail and keep going until it reached the station.

From the Cold Spring station, keeper Jim McNaughton and Jay Kelley saw an Appaloosa pony limping slowly down the mountain trail in the gathering twilight. It looked like a pack horse with the pack slipped far over to one side, but they knew the pony to be Bart's. And they knew only too well what the sagging pack would be. Mounting, they raced up the trail to meet the staggering pony and its burden. Bart's body hung from the saddle horn like a blood-soaked bag of grain, his head resting on his knee. At first they could not be sure that he was breathing, but there was a weak murmur of pulse in his wrist.

The men who made the Pony Express successful were too strong to be deterred by tragedy. As Jim McNaughton lifted Bart gently from the saddle, he told Kelley, "I'll get him back to the station and do what I can for him, Jay. You run that mail on through to Churchill. With night a-fallin' you can prob'ly make it all right."

Jay stripped the blood-streaked *mochila* from Bart's saddle and tossed it across his own. Jim McNaughton had barely turned down the trail with Bart in his arms before Jay raced past them, heading out on the 87-mile night ride to Fort Churchill.

All through the night Jim McNaughton sat at Bart's side, tending his wounds and trying to rouse him enough to swallow stimulants. Toward morning semiconsciousness returned, but only long enough for Bart to whisper a few words about the ambush. At dawn he roused again and mumbled, *"Diga al Señor Bob que guardé con mi vida."* (Tell Mr. Bob that I guarded it with my life.) Then the light flickered out for one of the bravest Mexican boys this country has ever known.

15

MANY BOOKS have been written about the Pony Express, and most of them name Buffalo Bill Cody as the greatest of all the riders. There is no doubt that Buffalo Bill was a great rider and frontiersman, but it is very doubtful that he ever carried the Pony Express mail. He did work for Russell, Majors & Waddell at that time, but he was then only fourteen years old, and worked as a messenger boy at Leavenworth, Kansas. The stories of his daring experiences as a Pony Express rider were never told until he became famous and had a talented publicity agent.

"Wild Bill" Hickok became most famous of all the men who worked on the Pony Express route, but he was not a rider. He was stableman at the Rock Creek station in eastern Nebraska. It was there that he gained his first fame — and the name of "Bill." One of the men whom he and his friend Doc Brink are said to have killed in self-defense gave him the name as well as the fame.

James Butler Hickok was twenty-three years old when he came from Illinois to take the job of stableman at Rock Creek. At that time he had no mustache to cover his buck teeth and protruding upper lip. Dave McCanles, a hard-drinking bully who had a homestead nearby, ridiculed Jim's appearance, laughed at him, and called him "Duckbill." After their famous gun fight, Jim was arrested, tried for murder, and exonerated. But the sheriff misunderstood the nickname. He wrote out his warrant for "Dutch Bill" Hickok. The "Dutch" was soon forgotten, but the "Bill" stuck.

No braver or more self-sacrificing group of men and boys was ever gathered for any undertaking than for the Pony Express. But standing out above them all was Pony Bob Haslam. After the punishment of a daylong run, many a Pony rider came into his home station a worn-out man, bleeding from mouth and nose. Jim Moore, Jay Kelley, Jack Keetley, and other boys made fabulous rides, but it was Pony Bob who seemed indestructible.

Bob Haslam's regular route was between Friday's Station on the California-Nevada line and Fort Churchill, but he rode wherever the danger and the need were greatest. During the first six weeks of the Pony Express, Bob was wounded twice by Indian arrows. Fortunately, both were flesh wounds, and he paid no more heed to them than a boy will pay to a cut finger. Without slowing his pace, he pulled the arrows out and kept on to the end of his route. By the time the next mail came in, he was back in the saddle and ready to go.

At dawn, a few days after Bart Riles was killed, Pony Bob rode into Reed's Station to find all the horses gone. He stopped only ten minutes to feed and water his tired pony, then rode the 15 miles to Fort Churchill, the end of his route. There he found the one exception among the Pony Express riders. The man who was to have taken the

mochila on eastward refused to make the dangerous ride over the Ambush Trail to Smith's Creek.

By chance, W. C. Marley, superintendent of
the Pony Express in western Nevada, was at the
station. After trying to persuade the frightened
man to make his ride, he turned to Pony Bob and
said, "Bob, the mail's got to go through. I'll give
you fifty dollars if you'll make this ride."

Pony Bob had just ridden 75 rugged miles, but
he didn't hesitate. "You've made a deal," he said.
"I'll go at once."

It took Bob just ten minutes to eat, clean his
rifle, load two extra cylinders for his revolvers,
and climb back into the saddle. He made the
run through the aspen thickets in Carson River
Marsh in record time. Out on the far side, he
stopped to rest his pony, picking a barren hilltop
where there was no chance of being ambushed.
Then he mounted and rode on. Four miles out-
side Stillwater, he found his way blocked by
a band of thirty Paiute warriors, all well mounted
and armed with good rifles. Among them was a
young chief who spoke a little English, and who
knew Bob Haslam's reputation.

Without hesitating, Bob looped the reins around his saddle horn, snatched the revolvers from his belt, cocked them, and spurred straight at the Indians. The young chief waved his warriors back frantically. As Pony Bob raced through the band, the chief shouted, "You pretty good fella — you go 'head!" Possibly the chief saved Bob's life, but it is certain that he saved the lives of at least three or four of his warriors.

At Stillwater, Bob chose the toughest mustang

in the corral, and rode on in the broiling sun for 20 waterless miles to Sand Springs. He spared his remount on the long climb up the Stillwater range, then made up time down the mountains and across the desert to Cold Spring — 87 miles out from Fort Churchill.

Night had fallen when Bob rode out of Cold Spring. Because of good luck, or his reputation, he had seen no Indians since the band had tried to block his way west of Stillwater. Ahead lay the 30 most treacherous miles on the route. Both relay stations had been burned, and midway to Smith's Creek — the end of his route — was Quaking Aspen Bottom.

Bob doubted that his luck could hold, but saved back enough of his pony's energy for a quick dash through the aspen thicket. Racing through, he could hear the Indians whooping and yelling, but they lacked the courage to block his way, and in the blackness he gave them no target to shoot at. At midnight he rode into Smith's Creek, turned the *mochila* over to Jay Kelley, and called it a day's work — 192 miles over the most dangerous trail on the continent, and with only two ten-minute breaks.

Pony Bob got nine hours' rest at Smith's Creek before the westbound mail was brought in. Then he set out for Cold Spring, saving his pony's strength for a fast sprint through Quaking Aspen Bottom. In the two-mile run through the aspens no shot was fired at him, and he heard no whooping from the Indians. To any other man this might have seemed good luck, but it worried Pony Bob.

Bob knew the Paiutes; if they had left their stronghold in the aspen thicket, they had gone to make an attack elsewhere. He had seen no sign of them along the trail from Smith's Creek, so they must be going to attack the stations to the west. He drove his pony hard on the climb to the top of the Desatoyas, then raced recklessly down the far side.

When Bob reached Cold Spring, he found his fears to be more than justified. The station had been raided, the keeper and his helper killed, and all the horses stolen. From the signs, Bob knew that the raid had been made soon after he passed the day before. That accounted for the whooping he had heard when he rode through Quaking Aspen Bottom. The Indians must then have been working themselves into a frenzy for the attack.

Knowing that the trail back to Smith's Creek was safe from Indian attack or ambush — and with his pony already tired from a 30-mile run — Bob might have been expected to turn back; but no such thought entered his mind. Tracks showed that the Indians, more than 100 strong, had taken the trail to the west. Since everything between had already been destroyed, their next attack was sure to be at Sand Springs, 37 miles farther on.

Scraping through the ruins, Bob found enough grain to feed his pony, gave it 20 minutes to eat and rest, then watered it and rode on. From Cold Spring he circled far to the south, around the Stillwater range. It would add 18 miles to his ride, but darkness was coming on, and the Indians might stop to camp before crossing the mountains. Besides, his pony was less apt to give out if it could be saved the hard climb over the range.

Anxious as he was to make time, Bob held his pony to a jogging trot. Until full darkness had fallen, he picked his way among the tallest sage-brush, keeping away from any bare spots where an Indian lookout on the mountains might spy him.

The moon was rising when Pony Bob circled the southern tip of the Stillwaters. From there his shortest route would have been straight across the desert to Sand Springs, but he turned his pony back to the north. Hugging close to the foot of the mountains, he kept his ears tuned sharply to every sound of the night. For half an hour he heard only the whinnying hoots of the screech owls, and the lonesome howl of the coyotes singing their evening song to the rising moon. Then came the sound he'd been waiting for. From high on the mountains came the far-off, deep-throated howl of a wolf.

Bob slid a hand along the pony's shoulder and patted its neck. "No need killin' yourself now, old-timer," he said. "Them Injuns is camped plumb astraddle of the pass, and old lobo wolf, he's callin' in the relatives to help haul down a bait o' Injun hoss meat for supper." Turning and guiding himself by the stars, he struck out for

Sand Springs in a beeline. The sky was graying in the east when he roused the keeper with a war-hoot.

The Sand Springs station was only a small adobe hut, with a feed shed and corral for the horses. There was no hope of defending it against a large Indian war party. The Stillwater station, 20 miles to the west, was a solidly built adobe fort, large enough to hold 20 men and 15 horses. Pony Bob wasted no time at Sand Springs. There was only one thing to be done, and he insisted that it be done quickly. Within a few minutes he was up on a fresh pony and, with the keeper and his helper, was driving the relay mounts across the desert toward Stillwater.

Although there was no time to lose, Bob moved carefully, spying out the desert ahead and keeping the loose horses well concealed in the sagebrush. There was recent Indian sign all the way, and he saw sentries posted on several hilltops, but slipped past them all without being seen. It was twilight when he raced the little herd of relay horses across the last stretch of barren ground and into the Stillwater corral.

At Stillwater, Bob found the keeper and 15 badly frightened emigrants barricaded in the station. They told him that ever since dawn a very strong war-band of Paiutes had been circling the station, well out of gunshot, and that an attack was expected at any minute. "Reckon you're as well off here as any place I can think of," Bob told them, "but I got a job o' work to get done. This here mail's past due at Churchill right now, and I aim to get it there as fast as the Lord'll let me."

As soon as full darkness fell, Bob rode out with the mail, and the Lord must surely have been with him. He made the 30-mile ride through Carson River Marsh in amazing time, and brought the mail into Fort Churchill only 3½ hours late. He was so tired that he took an hour-and-a-half nap before riding on 75 miles to Friday's Station, high in the Sierra Nevadas.

Altogether, Pony Bob Haslam had ridden 385 miles in a total of 78 hours, and with only 11 hours' rest. This was the greatest endurance record ever set by a Pony Express rider, but it was not Pony Bob's greatest ride.

16

Pony Bob Haslam's greatest ride — and possibly the greatest ride in American history — was made in March, 1861. By that time war between the North and South seemed certain, and California was still a very doubtful state. Whether it remained loyal to the Union or joined the Confederacy depended a great deal upon the policies set forth in Lincoln's inaugural address. California might swing to the cause of the Confederacy any day, and it was of the utmost importance that the address be relayed to Sacramento in the shortest possible time.

Weeks before the inauguration, Russell, Majors & Waddell made elaborate preparations for speeding the President's address to California. They spared no expense, hired hundreds of extra men, and arranged to have fresh relay horses waiting every ten miles along the whole 1966-mile route. Word was sent out to the Pony riders that horses were not to be spared under any conditions, that California might be lost to the Union if there was the slightest delay.

The Paiutes had made little trouble through the winter of 1860–61, and most of the Pony Express relay stations in Nevada had been rebuilt. But with the coming of spring the Indians again began their attacks. Stations were raided, and ambushes were set all along the 117-mile trail from Smith's Creek to Fort Churchill. It was no surprise when Bob Haslam was chosen to carry President Lincoln's address over this extremely hazardous route.

Pony Bob was waiting at Smith's Creek when the *mochila* bearing the President's address was brought in from the east. To lighten his horses' loads as much as possible, he discarded his rifle, but carried two Colt revolvers stuck under his belt. With a change of horses at Mount Airy, and another at Castle Rock, he made the fastest time ever ridden to Cold Spring. He was at first surprised, and then worried, when no Indians tried to ambush him in Quaking Aspen Bottom or at either of the mountain passes.

The fastest horse at the Cold Spring station was saddled and bridled when Bob raced in, but he insisted on riding Old Buck, a slower horse. The old buckskin was a desert mustang. As a colt he had been caught and broken by Indians, who must have abused him. He could smell Indians for miles across the desert, and he hated them as few horses can hate.

To the west of Cold Spring, the trail led through a desert valley, thickly dotted with clumps of sagebrush and greasewood, some of them higher than a mounted rider's head. This was a perfect place for an Indian ambush, and Pony Bob was sure that one would be set somewhere along the trail. He might have circled wide to avoid it, but this would have cost precious time. He touched spurs to Old Buck and put him straight down the trail at a brisk canter, watching the wise old mustang's ears as he rode.

Two miles out from the station, Buck raised his head quickly, pointed his ears straight ahead, and snorted. There was a very light breeze blowing from the west, and Bob knew it had brought the scent of Indians to Old Buck. He guessed, from the lightness of the breeze, that they would be about two miles away — and they would certainly have the trail ambushed. Bob slowed Buck's gait to an easy lope, looped the reins around the saddle horn, and drew his revolvers, cocking them and checking both cylinders.

A mile farther on, Buck began bobbing his head and snorting angrily. If the old mustang could have talked he couldn't have told Bob more plainly that Indians were close ahead and that there were many of them. There was still plenty of time to turn back safely, or to circle cautiously around the trap and avoid it, but Bob rode straight on, leaning forward to stroke the buckskin's neck. "Simmer down, old bird dog, simmer down," Bob whispered to him. "Keep that head up and them ears a-workin'. I'll need to know right plum where them varmints is at."

As if understanding what Bob had said, the old

buckskin stopped snorting, changed his gait to a shuffling, noiseless pace, and held his head high. Bob rose to his tiptoes in the stirrups, but could see nothing more than a sea of green-gray brush tops spread out across the desert. A quarter-mile farther on, Buck pointed his ears quickly to right and left, and the nerves twitched in his shoulders. This was it! Indians were flanked out on both sides of the trail — and there were lots of them. Pony Bob dropped flat along the mustang's neck, revolvers eye-high and spurs raking.

Ears tight back, yellow teeth bared, and muzzle stuck straight out, Old Buck turned on the speed. At the same moment the Paiute war shriek ripped the desert stillness to shreds. War-painted Indians boiled out of the brush like a swarm of ants. Rifle shots cracked from both sides, in front and behind. Arrows filled the air like straws in a hurricane. Bob held his fire, depending on the speed of his horse to take him through; but Old Buck fought back. Without breaking his pace, he snaked his head from side to side, slashing his teeth at any naked shoulder within reach.

This was no ordinary ambush. The Paiutes had

too often been outrun by swift Pony Express horses, and this time they had set their trap carefully. Pony Bob had no sooner burst through the main ambush then he found himself surrounded by mounted warriors — several of them on stolen Pony Express horses. One by one the Indian ponies fell back, but, on Old Buck, Bob couldn't hope to outrun the swift Express ponies.

Few men have ever had greater affection for fine horses than Pony Bob Haslam. But there was only one way to get out of this ambush, and he took it. He wasted no useless shots at Indians, hanging against the far side of their ponies and shooting under their necks. There were only twelve shots in his two revolvers, and he'd need every one of them. Holding his fire until an Express pony was within sure range beside him, Bob took careful aim for the heart and squeezed the trigger.

Three of the stolen ponies were down and three were left when an arrow ripped into the muscle of Bob's left arm, hit the bone and stood quivering. The arm dropped, useless, but Bob's fingers still clutched the half-empty revolver. The shock of the stone arrowhead against bone sent waves of pain through his whole body, but he didn't straighten up or stop spurring. Carefully slipping the gun from his right hand back under his belt, he jerked the arrow out, then reached down and took the other gun from his useless hand.

Seeing that Bob was wounded, the Indians howled like rabid wolves, but they had learned better than to ride abreast of him. Closing in behind, they pressed him hard, shooting arrow after arrow past his head and shoulders from close range.

Turning his head and taunting them — so as to keep them shooting at him rather than Old Buck — Pony Bob watched for the chance that might save him. It came sooner than he expected. At a place where the trail narrowed, the Indians strung out in close single file. Snapping upright and twisting in his saddle, Bob poured three quick shots at the forehead of the lead pony. It went down in a diving somersault. The second pony piled up on top of it, but the third swerved in time to race past.

Instantly Bob fell flat against Old Buck's neck,

tossed away his empty revolver and reached for the other. He had just yanked it from his belt and was turning back to fire when an arrow whanged past his face. It ripped through his lips, knocked out five front teeth, and fractured his jaw. For a moment or two blackness swirled before his eyes, but he didn't lose consciousness. Grabbing blindly for the saddle horn, he shook his head fiercely to clear his brain. The instant his sight cleared he whirled in the saddle and emptied his gun at the chest of the oncoming pony. Bob never knew whether or not the pony went down. It took all his attention to fight back the dizziness and pain that were muddling his brain. When his head cleared again, Buck was racing up the trail — alone — and the Middle Gate relay station was in sight, only a mile away.

When Old Buck galloped into Middle Gate, Bob Haslam was a frightening sight. At the fast pace they had been going, blood from his mouth had blown back to cover his whole face and chest. And his left arm, already swelling, hung at his side like a wet red log. Blood dripped from his fingertips as he jumped from the saddle, trying to pull the *mochila* off with him.

Both the stationkeeper and his helper, men in their fifties, wanted to carry the *mochila* on for Bob, but he wouldn't listen to them. Although, with his broken jaw and torn lips, he could hardly

make himself understood, he mumbled, "Fetch me a clean rag to hold in my mouth, and wrop up this arm. I'm a-goin' on through."

Pony Bob Haslam did go through — all the way to Fort Churchill. When he rode in, his wounded arm had swollen until it was bigger around than his thigh, and his face was almost unrecognizable. But in unbelievable time he had brought through the *mochila* holding President Lincoln's address — dripping with his own blood. Badly wounded and with one arm useless for most of the way, he had ridden 120 miles in 8 hours and 10 minutes, and had changed mounts 12 times.

That was the fastest trip ever made by the Pony Express. In just 7 days and 17 hours from the time President Lincoln's inaugural address was telegraphed from Washington to St. Joseph, a hard-spurring Pony rider galloped it into Sacramento, California.

With men such as Bob Haslam, Boston Upson, Jay Kelley, Bart Riles, Major Egan, and all the other great riders, it seems impossible that the Pony Express could have become useless in little more than a year and a half. But that is just what happened. In those 18 months the Pony Express riders carried the mail farther than 24 times around the world, but, fast as the ponies were, the progress being made in the United States was faster. While the Pony riders were racing across the prairies, mountains, and deserts, other men were setting poles and stringing telegraph wires between California and the Missouri River. On October 24, 1861, the telegraph line was completed, the first message sent from Washington to San Francisco, and the need for the Pony Express was ended.

Although the Pony Express was short-lived and lost its owners many thousands of dollars, it was far from being a failure. It had accomplished the two great tasks for which it had been established: it proved the Central Overland Route across the Rocky Mountains to be passable the year around — and California had remained in the Union. If, as some historians say, the riders of the Pony Express saved California for the Union, then our debt to them is greater than all our respect and admiration can ever pay.

INDEX

182